TEACHING STUDENTS WITH AUTISM in a Catholic Setting

TEACHING STUDENTS WITH AUTISM in a Catholic Setting

Lawrence R. Sutton, Ph.D.

LOYOLA PRESS.
A JESUIT MINISTRY
Chicago

LOYOLA PRESS.
A JESUIT MINISTRY

3441 N. Ashland Avenue
Chicago, Illinois 60657
(800) 621-1008
www.loyolapress.com

Cover art credit: Loyola Press
Back cover author photo, Warling Studios.

ISBN-13: 978-0-8294-4707-1
Library of Congress Control Number: 2019951136

Printed in the United States of America.
20 21 22 23 24 25 26 27 28 Versa 10 9 8 7 6 5 4 3 2

The splendor of the rose and the whiteness of the lily do not rob the little violet of its scent nor the daisy of its simple charm. If every tiny flower wanted to be a rose, spring would lose its loveliness.

—St. Thérèse of Lisieux

Contents

Foreword

In November 2014, the Vatican hosted an international conference on autism. I was among a handful of presenters to offer a pastoral perspective, with the majority focusing on research and cures. I shared the painful stories of parents who longed for their children with autism and other disabilities to attend Catholic schools and faith formation classes alongside their siblings and peers. I relayed these comments shared by parents in a poll conducted by the National Catholic Partnership on Disability (NCPD):

- "I attended Catholic school from kindergarten through college, became a Catholic school teacher and administrator, yet there is not a place in the Catholic school system for my son."
- "It is a sad experience when the pastor, priest, or lay leaders place insurmountable obstacles in the way of families with children with autism spectrum disorders."
- "The lack of a parish policy on inclusion in faith formation makes families feel hopeless."

I was pleased to be able to report to the Vatican audience that there were signs of hope amid the pain:

> Hope is being animated throughout the Americas in parishes that recognize the gifts and potential of each person. When parishes are open to responding to the real and perceived challenges raised by parishioners with autism and their families, the gifts and graces

> of the Holy Spirit are poured out in countless ways. When the parishioner with autism is seen as a valued member of the community rather than a problem to be solved, the entire parish is blessed and experiences anew the infinite love of God.

I further noted that "Catholic universities offer courses of study to train future teachers and catechists to work with students with disabilities."

Among the signs of hope in the U.S. Catholic Church is Deacon Larry Sutton, who inadvertently developed a catechetical model utilized in numerous parishes and dioceses in response to learning of the needs of two young men with autism who had been denied services at their own parishes. Deacon Larry did not set out to start a program, certainly not one that would become an international model. Rather he responded personally to the troubling exclusion experienced by two families. As a clinical psychologist, Sutton had worked with children and youth with autism at several schools and for the State of Pennsylvania Bureau of Autism Services. When confronted with these young men whose parents were seeking faith formation and sacramental preparation for their sons, Sutton applied his vast knowledge and experience in serving individuals with autism, as well as his deaconate training, to develop a unique methodology that incorporates peer mentors, as well as a support system for parents. Sutton also stresses the need for the students to be actively engaged in the life of their parish community, echoing the guidance provided by the U.S. Catholic bishops in their 2017 Revised Edition of the *Guidelines for the Celebration of the Sacraments with Persons with Disabilities*[1] (Guiding Principle #5): "Parish catechetical and sacramental preparation programs may need to be adapted for some parishioners with disabilities, though, as much as possible, persons with disabilities

1 *Guidelines for the Celebration of the Sacraments with Persons with Disabilities*, Revised Edition, United States Conference of Catholic Bishops, Washington, DC, 2017. Used with permission. All rights reserved.

should be integrated into the ordinary programs. They should not be segregated for specialized catechesis unless their disabilities make it impossible for them to participate in the basic catechetical program. Even in those cases, participation in parish life is encouraged in all ways possible."

In *Teaching Students with Autism in a Catholic Setting*, Sutton again applies his knowledge and experience to provide valuable guidance to teachers and administrators in Catholic schools. His advice can equally assist catechists and catechetical leaders seeking to serve diverse learners in faith formation classes. Throughout the book, Sutton provides helpful examples of real students who experience problems and success in the classroom. He provides a basic understanding of what autism is and is not. He explains a number of important concepts including executive functioning, theory of mind, and intellectual functioning. Each chapter provides very practical direction and techniques to aid teachers or catechists in understanding the importance of rules and structure, how to analyze problem behaviors, the value of visual schedules, the crucial need to work with parents, and six specific ways in which they can increase control of their classrooms.

Several years ago, I was invited by a pastor to speak with all of his staff about how to create a parish where individuals with disabilities and their families truly experience a sense of belonging and welcome. After I had commended the parish on the excellent efforts already underway, I was asked by one participant why my talk was even needed if they were already doing a good job in creating access. I turned to the pastor for an answer to his assistant, and I will never forget his thoughtful response: "I do not want anyone who approaches our parish to hear 'No.' They need to know they are welcome here."

Despite much progress in recent years, parents are still longing for their children to be included in Catholic schools or programs of faith formation. All too often they still hear "No, we cannot accommodate you." This, of course, is understood as, "You are not welcome at this parish." Through this very helpful book, Sutton has provided a great service to assist in bringing the goal of full participation to fruition in the lives of countless families by equipping school administrators, teachers, and catechists with the tools needed for them to confidently say, "Yes, you are most welcome here."

Janice L. Benton, ofs

Introduction

Early in my career I worked for the DePaul Institute, which is now the DePaul School for Hearing and Speech, a private school for children who were deaf or hard of hearing. Using the oral method, children learned to speech-read others for receptive communication and to verbally speak for expressive communication. It was at DePaul that I first learned the meaning of *functional communication*: to be able to communicate to another what it was that one needed and to respond to someone else by doing what that one asked.

Although my primary role at DePaul was to offer counseling and to conduct psychological evaluations, I was also able to observe how children learned to use language. One of the techniques that impressed me the most was the way a teacher would hold an object next to her mouth so that the child could see the object and see how the mouth formed the word representing the object. This essentially impressed a picture on the word being heard, and through amplification of whatever hearing the child had, to hear how the word was stated. The method was remarkably successful.

When I left the DePaul Institute after many years, I began working with children with autism. I worked for the Watson Institute, which had a clinic and a school. Although my primary role was again to provide counseling and to conduct psychological evaluations, I had the opportunity to observe children in class, at play, and during nonstructured times at lunch and recess. I saw firsthand how a simple picture card, or a small group of them (a Picture Exchange Card or PEC program), meant the difference between children being able to communicate what they wanted and children having meltdowns because they could not communicate their needs to another. I could observe firsthand the methods employed and how the PEC system worked in real life. That is, I witnessed how aggressive tantrum behaviors could be modified or shaped to something much less aggressive because of the consistency of the methods used.

Part of the school services that Watson provided was an integrated preschool program referred to as LEAP (**L**earning **E**xperiences: an **A**lternative **P**rogram). In this program, children with autism attended a typical preschool with neurotypical children (children without autism) who served as models for how to do various everyday preschool activities, functions, and behaviors. It was my initial experience at seeing firsthand *peer modeling* used with children with autism.

Over the course of the following years I began working with private schools, Catholic and non-religious, who teach children with and without autism. In these schools, I have been able to learn teaching methods and techniques that have led to success in educating children and teens with autism. In each grade at our Lady of Grace School in my home parish, I saw the value of carefully pairing a peer mentor (a neurotypical child) with a child who has autism to help the child with autism succeed not only academically but also, to a large extent, socially. Most impressively, I was able to shadow the amazing integrated program at the St. Madeleine Sophie School, near Seattle, which helped to build the personal confidence and academic achievement of children with a variety of disabilities, including autism.

My purpose in writing this book is to share with the Catholic schoolteacher information, successful methods, and best practices to educate children with autism and other developmental disabilities. I would like teachers to be comfortable teaching children who may learn differently.

I also want to illustrate and highlight several Catholic schools in different parts of the United States that are thriving by incorporating our Catholic values to both educate children with autism and to increase the quality of life for these exceptional children, their families, and our communities. Finally, I would like to provide educators with a list of resources for their continued learning, growth, and development.

1

Students Who Learn Differently

As a body is one though it has many parts, and all the parts of the body, though many, are one body, so also Christ. For in one Spirit we were all baptized into one body, whether Jews or Greeks, slaves or free persons, and we were all given to drink of one Spirit. . . . But God has so constructed the body as to give greater honor to a part that is without it, so that there may be no division in the body, but that the parts may have the same concern for one another. If [one] part suffers, all the parts suffer with it; if one part is honored, all the parts share its joy.

—1 Corinthians 12:12–13, 24–26

The Learner with Autism and the Catholic School

Educating someone with autism doesn't need to be difficult. Students with autism are similar to neurotypical students in many ways. Children with autism, for example, are often proficient problem solvers. They can also have preferred areas of interest and are good in some subjects and not so good in others. However, many students are easily affected by the environment around them. These students seem to learn differently from neurotypical learners.

Many learners with autism can (and do) grow up and develop friendships with their peers and can lead happy, productive lives as adults. Sometimes having this disorder may overshadow the gifts that each learner likely has. Because of the wide nature of autism as a spectrum disorder, one person with autism could have a limited intellectual ability while another could be gifted intellectually; one may understand mathematics after only one explanation and quickly become bored when repetitive problems are assigned to them, while another might struggle and seem never to understand a mathematical concept. Some children with autism excel in mathematics, others in science or in art. As with every child, each individual is different.

Learners with autism don't always recognize the connection between similar ideas and objects. Therefore, they appear to be more concrete learners, often applying one concept to another without recognizing the differences in context, or they cannot make the connection between two similar concepts. In this way, they may seem to lack insight and may appear to lack abstract thinking processes. Moreover, they may appear as if they *should* know something because of its similarity to another concept when they clearly don't. For example, some young learners may learn that two plus two equals four, but don't recognize and need to learn that three plus one equals four as well. In a similar sense, many individuals with autism find it difficult when similar sounding words have different meanings, such as the word *read,* which sounds similar to *red.* Both sound the same in some contexts (I *read* the book or the *red* book), but, as they cannot generalize concepts well, those with autism need to learn the specific rules for the use of a word as opposed to other words that sound the same when they have two or more meanings independently.

The Call for Inclusion and Belonging

As a Catholic community, we are called to recognize and respond to those around us as children of God, regardless of race or culture, ability or disability. This call for inclusion is clearly expressed by the United States Conference of Catholic Bishops,

> The Church continues to affirm the dignity of every human being, and to grow in knowledge and understanding of the gifts and needs

> of her members who live with disabilities. Likewise, the Church recognizes that every parish community includes members with disabilities, and earnestly desires their active participation. All members of the Body of Christ are uniquely called by God by virtue of their Baptism. In light of this call, the Church seeks to support all in their growth in holiness, and to encourage all in their vocations. Participating in, and being nourished by, the grace of the sacraments is essential to this growth in holiness. Catholic adults and children with disabilities, and their families, earnestly desire full and meaningful participation in the sacramental life of the Church. (*Guidelines for the Celebration of the Sacraments with Persons with Disabilities,* June 2017)

Catholic children with autism and other developmental disabilities, by virtue of their baptism, have the right to a meaningful Catholic education. God has given each Catholic man, woman, and child gifts that need to be nurtured and supported so as to allow them to reach their fullest potential. The United States Conference of Catholic Bishops (USCCB) wrote,

> All persons with disabilities have the capacity to proclaim the Gospel and to be living witnesses to its truth within the community of faith and offer valuable gifts. Their involvement enriches every aspect of Church life. They (persons with disabilities) are not just recipients of catechesis—they are also its agents. (*The National Directory for Catechesis,* 2005)

And as agents and persons of dignity, these children must be given special attention and protection. Although statistics vary, one in five children experience some form of bullying behavior before they graduate high school. If a child has a disability, such as autism spectrum disorder, his or her likelihood of being bullied is up to three times higher, according to the U.S. Department of Health and Human Services. Children with disabilities are children, with the same rights and privileges as their neurotypical counterparts, and these same children also have hopes, wishes, and dreams that need to be supported, nurtured, and encouraged. As children of God ourselves, should we not support each of our sisters and brothers—children of God as well?

Children with disabilities fortunately have champions like Pope Francis, who has called us to "speak up for those who cannot speak for themselves, for the rights of all who are destitute" (Proverbs 31:8, NIV). We are called to "speak up and judge fairly and to defend the rights of the poor and needy" (31:9, NIV). We need to not only recognize when injustices are being made to those with disabling conditions but also act to correct them and to help prevent similar acts from ever occurring again.

As a church, as a Christian community, we need to understand and recognize the gifts and strengths of all its members and to overtly and meaningfully act to meet, prepare, and include each of its members by serving its children and adults with disabilities. In effect, we are serving all God's people through some of its more vulnerable members. The result is a powerful form of *evangelization of the family.*

As so eloquently stated by Cardinal Peter Turkson at the World Autism Awareness Day in Vatican City on April 2, 2018,

> The Church, in her works, bears witness to her care and concern for persons with autism spectrum disorders. There is a general attitude of acceptance in our communities, even if one struggles to practice a true inclusion, which is why it is fundamental that our Christian communities be 'houses' in which every form of suffering finds compassion, in which every family with its burden of pain and toil may feel understood and respected in its dignity.

Cardinal Turkson went on to say,

> It is essential to actively stand beside those who are affected by autism spectrum disorders and their families, upon whom weighs an enormous and sometimes unbearable amount of work. Their displays of distress and their calls for help should be heard and transformed into concrete and appropriate actions and activities. All family members must be taken into consideration, not only parents but also any other children, whose development requires the utmost attention and care. How often do they experience a feeling of inadequacy, ineffectiveness, and frustration!

In addition to this, Pope Francis affirms in his November 22, 2014 address to the XXIX International Conference sponsored by the Pontifical Council for Health Care Workers,

> Everyone should be committed to promoting acceptance, encounter, and solidarity through concrete support and by encouraging renewed hope, thereby contributing to overcome the isolation and, in many cases, the stigma to which people with autism spectrum disorders are also subjected, and often their families too.

The Challenge to Catholic Schools

Given the multiple calls to action by church leaders and Pope Francis, Catholic schools are challenged to meet the needs of those with disabilities. This act is not something that is "nice to do"; it is something that we are "called to do." Catholic schools must serve both the faith community and the community at large through teaching its children to contribute to the common good as active and caring members of society.

With the dramatic numbers of those diagnosed with autism (according to the Centers for Disease Control and Prevention, one in every fifty-nine students age eight years in the United States falls on the spectrum), parents of children with autism are seeking the safety, structure, and spiritual benefits of safe peer models offered in local Catholic schools.

Possibly due to a lack of understanding and/or an inability to intuitively understand social rules and norms, the student with autism must rely upon similar-aged peers to know what to do in social situations. Catholic schools can and are responding to these needs, as well as academic challenges, but require the intellectual and physical resources to consistently provide the best possible care and education for children with disabilities. This means working with qualified professionals, educating teachers on how they can best serve children with autism spectrum disorders and other disabilities, and informing parents about ways they can join in the effort to best serve these children. It also means allocating or raising the funds, modifying the school grounds, and designing new spaces to adequately serve all students, including those with autism and other disabilities.

These intellectual and physical resources may include a working understanding of how students with autism communicate, both to express what they know and to successfully express that they are encountering problems when they occur. It is important to remember that students with autism often use their *behavior as a form of communication*. That is to say, when they do not understand, or when material is presented too quickly for them to process, the children may become frustrated and upset and "meltdown", an innate way the body expresses a need for assistance when a person is overwhelmed. In other words, a meltdown is a loss of control due to an overload of stimulus. The child does not have power over it.

This is not an indication that the children don't want to learn. Understanding students with autism isn't necessarily difficult, but it involves knowing the children, knowing how they solve problems, understanding what they know and what they don't know, and how they communicate. Further, these resources may require a coordinated effort to proceed with both intention and purpose so that the educational efforts can be successful. In this regard, coordinated efforts sometimes require resources and training that heretofore may not have been traditionally accessible to typical Catholic schools. Some programming options within the realm of Catholic schools that could be used to obtain these resources will be illustrated within this book.

I will share several real-life case examples to highlight specific challenges that students with autism may encounter in learning and strategies on how to address these problems. We will begin with the story of Mark to illustrate some of the more common struggles and questions many students with autism face as they enter and proceed through elementary and secondary education. It is important to remember that autism, if diagnosed correctly, is a *lifelong disorder*. Because of delays in the development of executive functioning and recognition of the Theory of Mind perspective of the children with autism (see chapter 2), each new experience encountered typically requires a new script or a new process on what to do or how to proceed as the student with autism often isn't capable of correctly generalizing one newly learned rule or script to a similar experience.

Mark Enters School

It's six-year-old Mark's first day of school. He's very excited. He's wearing his favorite shirt, which is bright and colorful. Although it still has a few stains from Christmas last year, the shirt is one of Mark's prized possessions. Mom is still not allowed to wash it, and he's wearing his favorite socks, too. It's taken him a long time to get dressed because it's been hard for Mark to put on his socks. Socks are kind of hard because Mark won't let his mom wash his favorite pair. Also, the seams on the other socks don't seem to line up across the tops of his toes. This causes Mark discomfort. Yet, though it takes a while, Mark eventually does get his socks and shoes on.

Mark is finally ready to go and arrives at school just after the bell rings. But that's okay as it's just the first day. Mom walks him into the classroom. There, the teacher greets her with a big smile and then turns her attention to Mark. The teacher introduces herself. Mark, however, doesn't make eye contact, though it is apparent he has heard the greeting. Instead, Mark looks toward the window and then toward the busy wall and then toward the wooden train next to the window. Mark loves trains. But then the teacher starts to touch Mark and then takes Mark by the hand and points to what will be his work area. It includes a table and some chairs. The teacher helps Mark into his seat.

The room is fascinating. There're so many things to look at. On the wall there are these big letters with colorful pictures under each one. And there's a fish tank in the back of the room. Then there is the window, and it's a hot day, and the windows are open, and I can

hear the cars and the playground; there must be kids outside, a lot of kids, and then there is that wooden train under the window. . . .

The teacher must have done something. . . . Where did everybody go? I'm sitting by myself; they are all in the front of the room sitting in a circle. Is she calling me?

But all I hear are those kids on the playground. I wonder what they're doing. Now she's holding my arm. She's touching me again. I don't like being touched. She's pulling me! I'm starting to get upset, and I don't want to get upset.

I'm almost having a meltdown, but she's telling me to sit. She makes me sit, and she starts to read a story . . . and I start to look around. I stop crying as she reads and I get up from the circle because I see something on the blackboard. I wonder. . . . I go up and I start to touch it. Wait, she's there again holding my arm. She's pulling me back to the floor, and I start to cry again, and now I'm screaming and hitting and kicking and—and now I really am in a meltdown.

Mark goes into a meltdown. His mom is called—the child is inconsolable—and she comes to take him home. So ends Mark's first day of school.

This is a story of Mark, a first-grade student who has a high-functioning form of an autism spectrum disorder. He loves reading and numbers. Mark comes into first grade with the ability to read short books. He's been sight-reading words since he was three years old. He can also do simple and moderately difficult elementary mathematic problems. Mark doesn't know what to do when he is bored. He is easily distracted. He is also interested in many things in his new classroom, including the desks, the wall furnishings, and the SMART board. Mark is also restless and wants to explore his new room. Mark is hypersensitive and often averse to being touched. He has a severe sensitivity to noise. He has many other sensitivities as well, including lighting and certain textures

(such as smooth or grainy surfaces on desks), which can distract him from the task at hand, but his teacher doesn't know any of this.

Because Mark has not been formally diagnosed with autism, his teacher sees him as a child who is easily distracted and often disrupts her class. This means he is a child who requires a great deal of focused, one-on-one attention. It would have been critical for Mark as well as for his new teacher (and the school) that Mark's parents met with his teacher days, or even weeks, before the first day of class. Although his parents could not have alerted the teacher to his disability, since Mark had not been formally diagnosed with autism spectrum disorder, they could have used that opportunity to share their observations of his behaviors and sensitivities when he was at home or playing with a similar aged child. Then preparations could have been made to ease Mark into his new environment. Further, arrangements could have been made for Mark to visit his new classroom before there were other students in it and, ideally, before there were so many adornments on the walls.

Summary

Is Mark an isolated case? Chances are, no. Why, though, would Mark's parents not share with his teacher his medical and developmental concerns before school started? Some parents may be afraid that if a teacher knew their son or daughter had autism, the school would reject their child.

With recognition that, as a form of communication, a behavior might be trying to express a question, a call for clarity, or simply a call for help, a Catholic school teacher can and should meaningfully help a child with autism to develop the gifts that God has given to him/her. It is a different way of looking at a new student entering a school, entering an individual classroom—although this child might be very bright, his or her sensory and processing problems may present challenges that are different from more "typical" students, thus creating a different type of challenge for the Catholic school teacher.

2

What Is Autism?

This picture shows a group of students looking with rapt attention at a teacher reading a book. Do you see the girl in the foreground sitting off to the side holding the book? She finds it difficult to sit with the group, but she's very interested in the story. She may want to join the group eventually, but the girl can't sit still for long periods of time. She needs to move around and to be active. She needs to hold things in her hands as she is so restless.

If you see a candle flickering on the altar or hear beautiful music coming from the organ or, say, from a beautiful bird, you may very well feel moved emotionally. You may smile or join in song, or maybe pull out a notebook and write a journal line or two about the experience. If you're a child with autism though, you may *stim* (short for *self-stimulation*), that is, jump up and down, wave your fingers or hands, rock, or do some other form of self-stimulation to express your happiness. A child with autism may also stim when he or she is sad, restless, or bored. It is a learned way to express or manage emotions.

Characteristics of Autism

Autism is a developmental disorder and is often referred to as a spectrum disorder. This means that symptoms range from relatively mild to very severe. Autism disorders are diagnosed by observing a child's behaviors and development during early childhood years. Autism is presently a *lifelong disorder* that, as of today, cannot be cured. But if correctly diagnosed, autism can be successfully managed—in many cases—in such a way as to increase the child's quality of life and help him or her develop personal interests and God-given talents. There are currently no blood tests or screenings to identify whether autism is present in a toddler.

The etiology of autism is not clear. Autism may be caused by genetic mutations, or it may be a condition that is triggered by environmental factors. It is no longer considered a rare condition. According to the Centers for Disease Control and Prevention, about one in every fifty-nine eight-year-old children among a sample taken in 2014 was affected by autism. The disorder is four times more prevalent in boys than girls.

Autism is a developmental disability that manifests itself in early childhood, and it is diagnosed by the observation of poor *social skills*, limited and or confused *communication*, *repetitive behaviors*, and a limited range of *social interest and activities* when the individual is a *toddler*.

It is important to note that autism is not a mental illness or a psychiatric disorder (See "What Autism Is *Not*" later in this chapter for further explanation). Biological and neurological factors are likely at play here. Hence, many doctors and researchers see autism as a genetic condition. Most children or adults with autism do not need medication, psychotherapy, or psychiatric treatment. They need help managing aspects of their lives as they interact with the world around them.

Although the symptoms of autism vary with each person, there are some common traits. Many of these are illustrated in the case of Antonio, the young man whom I first got to know professionally as a psychologist and later in an adaptive religious-education program. Antonio's early development seemed to progress more slowly than other children of the same age. He didn't respond to verbal cues very well, and he didn't seem to look at his mother very much as an infant or toddler. Antonio didn't talk right away, and he didn't say his first words until he was nearly nine years of age.

Developmentally, it took his parents a while to realize that *something wasn't right*. Antonio was their first child, and like many new parents, they didn't have much contact with other children of Antonio's age to provide a comparison. First, because of Antonio's lack of language and responsiveness, they took Antonio to an audiologist when he was about two years old to see if he had a hearing problem. But they discovered that he didn't seem to have a hearing problem. Then they took him to a speech and language pathologist because he wasn't talking. Soon thereafter, Antonio was diagnosed with autism.

Since he didn't talk or use another form of expressive language, Antonio would express his frustration at not being understood by banging his head on the floor or kitchen table and then screaming. Sometimes he would strike his face with a closed fist. The blows didn't seem to hurt him. Antonio exhibited, at first blush, a high tolerance for pain.

When Antonio finally began communicating verbally, at around age eight or nine, he responded very slowly. His parents, a teacher, or another child would ask a question, but it would take Antonio a long time to answer, sometimes as long as ninety seconds. When the answer finally came, it was usually correct, but often the other person, frustrated because of having to wait so long, walked away and wasn't around to hear his answer. With his language impairment, Antonio couldn't take standardized intelligence tests or achievement tests in school. His teachers thought his intelligence was low, and they tried to steer him into a *life-skills curriculum* to learn basic daily-living skills. His parents, however, insisted that Antonio receive what they referred to as a "normal" or typical school education.

Antonio came to my religious-education program when he was fourteen years old. His faith mentor was a bright high school freshman. In an early class, the student asked Antonio if he ever received the sacrament of reconciliation and the Eucharist. Antonio responded, "Do you mean confession?" and then quickly added, "Do you mean like Cain and Abel?" To the astonishment of both his father and myself, Antonio then proceeded in a slow, methodical, and fluid way to tell the story of Cain and Abel from the Old Testament. I had been Antonio's psychologist for ten years, and this was the first time I had heard him say more than a few consecutive words at a time. His father stated that he had no idea how Antonio knew the story of Cain and Abel, for neither he nor Antonio's mother had ever told him the story. Up to that point, he had never participated in the parish religious-education program and, frankly, never attended Mass. None of us had any idea how a boy who was thought to have significant intellectual disability could seemingly *pull this story out of thin air*, so to speak, and express it in a fluid way. The impetus seemed to be his young mentor's question about the sacrament of reconciliation.

Antonio's story illustrates something that I will say often in this book: Some individuals with an autism spectrum disorder are usually unable to understand what's going on in other people's minds, but the reverse is also true. We don't always know what's going on in the minds of people with autism. Antonio reminded me how important it is, in my interactions with people with autism, to fully express my thoughts in complete sentences and to explain things clearly, even if the person doesn't give me any feedback that he's understood or even heard what I may have said. Whether or not the person in question is looking at me or listening, people with autism often know and understand much more than we think they do.

Antonio didn't receive the sacrament of Confirmation until the age of twenty. Over the course of the six years he was in the program, Antonio learned about the gifts of the Holy Spirit and was able to explain them and, to some extent, was able to say what it meant to be an adult in the Catholic Church. At the time of his confirmation, Antonio was able to recite common prayers and was participating in some small-group activities, even though he still preferred to spend time by himself. He was able to go to Mass each week, and he appeared to understand the rituals. He received the Eucharist regularly. Antonio is now an active and involved member of his parish.

Autism as an Information-Processing Disorder

Autism is a disorder that, in part, affects the brain's ability to process information. Sometimes sensory data gets jumbled, or a person's ability to understand language is impaired. Sometimes people with autism aren't able to make sense of verbal and nonverbal cues. Consequently, someone with autism does not easily recognize emotional responses and body language, which make up the subtle web of social interactions in which we all live.

Social Skills

Without direction or teaching in new or novel situations, children and teens with autism typically show a limited ability to respond to and interact with others. They often don't know or understand how to initiate and engage in simple social back-and-forth exchanges. Children with autism typically play alone. They often can't anticipate or draw logical, parallel conclusions or deductions because of deficits in executive functioning. They often lack the ability to connect past experiences with present actions or to plan and organize what to do next. As a consequence, they rarely have success in reaching out to others, at least when they are very young.

Communication Skills

Delayed and impaired language development is another characteristic of autism. Some people with autism never develop functional language; that is, they never cultivate the ability to fully understand what others are communicating to them or the ability to fully express their own needs and wants. The majority of individuals with autism have limited vocabularies. Even those capable of complex speech show abnormalities such as echolalia (repeating words spoken by others), unconventional word use, unusual inflection, and mumbling or repeating to themselves what someone else has said before responding. Many times, they speak in a monotone. As noted earlier, people with autism typically have difficulty with nonverbal communication such as eye contact and body language in addition to reading facial, nonverbal, and social cues.

Rigid and Restricted Behavior

Children and teens with autism typically have narrow and unusual interests. For example, Antonio reads obsessively about the Revolutionary War. He can recite from memory precise details about battles and name the officers involved in specific battles. If left on his own, he would talk about specific battles from the war until he expressed every detail he had in his brain. Many children with autism also follow rigid routines and can become quite upset when these routines are disrupted or changed, particularly if there is no warning or if the change is made at the last minute.

Sensory Sensitivity

Many children with autism have numerous sensory problems. For instance, they are picky eaters because of the texture or smell of the food. Individuals with autism can be bothered by certain fabrics, tags, and seams in clothing. They can be highly sensitive to noise, piercing sounds, and even music. When they become adolescents, these sensory problems seem to change and require new techniques to manage them.

Stimming

As noted earlier, *stim* is short for *self-stimulation*. A stim is an expression or method that expresses happiness, sadness, excitement, or a variety of other emotions when an individual can't use expressive language. Self-stimulation can often be self-perpetuating. What may have initially excited a child—for instance, someone bouncing a bright red ball—may have ended, but the child's stimming has kept him or her in an excited state. The stimming behavior may continue long after the ball is nowhere in sight.

Typical stimming behaviors include hand flapping, shaking fingers in front of their eyes repetitively, bouncing up and down on their toes, rocking back and forth, and making specific types of noise. Stimming often functions as a form of communication, a way to express frustration, happiness, and/or excitement. It is also a reaction to stress. Children with autism, as noted earlier, are often hypersensitive to sights and sounds, and their ability to process sensory data appears to be faulty. So they relieve the apparent anxiety and confusion they feel by stimming.

Over time, I have found that children who stim at Mass, for example, provide constructive feedback, especially when I am preaching. As a deacon, I find it is often difficult to receive genuine or real-time feedback from neurotypical adults on how a sermon I'm giving is being received. However, this is often not the case with a child who has autism. I know my sermon is good when the church is quiet and one could figuratively hear a pin drop. But when my preaching is not so good, a child with autism in my parish will often get up and start pacing in front of the altar. But it is when a second child with autism stands and begins flapping his hands that I recognize I need to wrap the sermon up, for it's likely that I've lost the congregation. You see, many children with autism don't know that it's not polite to tell a cleric that they are boring or confusing when they preach. Ironically, by using very clear nonverbal methods, a child with autism clearly communicates what most members of the congregation—those who are "too polite"—are likely thinking at the time. Namely, that I am too boring today and have lost my audience.

Boundaries

Individuals with autism don't seem to intrinsically recognize social rules or boundaries; they need to be taught these rules. They don't start out intending to be mean or disrespectful; they are trying to be clear and concrete in what they are attempting to communicate. Often, however, their actions or words are misinterpreted and are thought to be mean or disrespectful. In truth, sometimes they are giving brutally honest feedback. This is why functional communication is the first and most important goal for most children with autism when they enter school.

Many children with autism have a limited understanding of social boundaries. For example, one child might not realize how close he is standing to someone, while another child might not understand the importance of letting someone else finish speaking before she starts talking herself. Communication is complicated, even for people without autism; active and mature communication includes both verbal and nonverbal language and rules for social interaction that change depending on a given situation.

Teaching social boundaries can be difficult. Many children with autism who have received medical and/or therapeutic services when they were toddlers, seemingly have no boundaries. They were likely dressed and undressed by others, had soiled clothing changed by others, and were bathed by others. As a result of constant contact with a parent or another caregiver, some children with autism may not know that it is not acceptable to interrupt a teacher or change the subject of a conversation midstream. Moreover, many people with autism don't realize they may make another person feel uncomfortable when their personal space is invaded. Children and teens with autism often have to be taught boundaries through role-playing and practice. Though verbal explanations can help sometimes, most children learn better through hands-on practice.

Intellectual Functioning

The fact that autism is a developmental disorder means in part that the child was born with something that is different from a typical child.

With regards to intelligence, the word *disorder* does not necessarily mean impaired. For example, a child with Down syndrome might have the developmental functioning level of a six-year-old across all skill levels, including social, language, and behavioral areas. That functioning level will persist throughout his or her lifetime. A person with autism, however, can have a low functioning level in some areas and average or even above-average functioning in others. These skills are often referred to as "splinter" skills. Some individuals with autism seem to have remarkable, savant-like or gifted abilities in one or more skill areas. For example, he or she might not be able to carry on a simple conversation about a classroom game, but when asked, can name all the players on the roster of all thirty teams in Major League Baseball. Another child might be able to perform complex mathematical calculations rapidly without use of paper or a calculator and yet struggle with simple reading.

This variant functioning is often part of the reason for much heartache and frustration for parents and others who interact with people with autism. They may think, *If he can talk about cars with such detail, why doesn't he talk to me when I ask him a question? If he can multiply five-digit numbers in his head, why doesn't he respond when his mother hugs him?* Some people with autism cannot perform these seemingly simple social and emotional interactions. The disability is developmental; something is lacking that cannot be readily supplied. They have to learn explicitly the skills that you and I have developed instinctually. People with autism can learn to compensate for their impairments, often by carefully following scripted behaviors and modeling, but this requires focused and intentional intervention.

Theory of Mind

Theory of Mind is the ability to understand that other people have beliefs, desires, attitudes, and feelings that are different from one's own. It is called a theory because the mind isn't directly observable. However, each of us has an intuitive understanding that we have a mind. In typical development, children develop a theory that other people have minds, too. We cannot have fully intimate relationships without it.

Theory of Mind abilities are typically impaired in people with autism. Often, individuals with autism have difficulty grasping that others think differently than they do. They don't understand that the things that happen to them may happen to other people too, and that other people may be happy, sad, frustrated, and excited as a result of those occurrences. This impairment is the source of the self-centeredness often observed in people with autism. They are quite literally stuck on themselves. Theory of Mind is the basis for empathy. Individuals with autism struggle at times with recognizing that others may have thoughts and feelings of their own, and so they struggle with empathy and typically don't know how to express it and need to be taught it.

People with autism seem to assume that everyone else shares their experiences. They feel that they don't have to explain anything because they assume that we already know exactly what they are thinking. For example, an adult with autism won't feel the need to explain why he is late for work because he will assume his boss knows already. A child will assume she won't have to tell her mother why she is angry because her mother should know. A boy will assume that everyone is as interested as he is in the rosters of Major League Baseball teams or in the details of Civil War battles, because that is his personal and preferred interest. People with autism often think everyone around them is omniscient.

In some ways, to a person with autism, we are omniscient to a certain degree. You and I mind-read all the time. We read faces and basic cues from body language, and we attend to the nuances of tone when other people are speaking. We read one another, so to speak, and react accordingly, which is shown by whether or not we smile, frown, laugh, or speak. Imagine what life is like for someone who can't do this. People with autism might talk endlessly about their favorite topic long past the point at which a polite listener has communicated in a dozen nonverbal ways that it's time to move on to something else. They may laugh at a funeral, fail to say thank you for gifts, or get angry when they are called for dinner, because they don't understand what is socially expected.

Social life is chaotic and painful for people with Theory of Mind deficits, so they learn coping strategies. One of these strategies is the ability to adhere to rules and routines. When you don't know what's expected of you, clinging to an established routine makes life more predictable and less chaotic. People with autism often develop highly detailed rules for their routines and become very upset when they are asked to alter them. Another coping strategy is imitation. People with autism who have Theory of Mind deficits will imitate what others do in social situations. This strategy may help in their interactions, but because the person with autism doesn't understand the nuances of social behavior, imitation is only a partial solution at best. I once witnessed an embarrassing example after a baptism. A man with autism observed carefully as family members came up to the mother of the newly baptized child and greeted her with hugs and kisses. The man was not part of the woman's immediate family and had never met her. Nevertheless, he approached the woman and tried to kiss and hug her; he was shocked when she pushed him away. He had made a mistake in guessing that hugging and kissing the mother of the newly baptized child is something *everyone* should do at a baptism.

Executive Function

Another characteristic of people with autism is the impairment of executive function. Executive function is considered the cognitive ability to control and regulate certain behaviors, such as recognizing how to begin or interrupt certain actions. Executive function allows one to anticipate an outcome and to adapt a routine to changing situations. Forming concepts and thinking abstractly are often considered components of executive function, including the ability to remember things such as the order of events and sequences, problem solving, reasoning, as well as effective use of language.

Executive function allows people to think abstractly. It is the ability to be flexible and adapt to changing conditions. Many people with autism that have impaired executive function systems have difficulty understanding cause and effect. They do not recognize that something they do in one moment may have an impact on later events. This makes it very difficult for them to set goals or organize any kind of plan for the future. They seem to have difficulty generalizing from one learned concept to a similar one. A child might know that it is dangerous to cross the street he lives on without a parent with him, but may think it is fine to cross the street his school is on, which has much more traffic, because no one has cautioned him about the danger present in that context. This impairment of executive function also makes establishing and maintaining social relationships difficult. A boy with autism who has a romantic crush on a classmate might not be deterred when she tells him to go away on one day, for every day is a new day. He might approach her again and again, not understanding that a firm rebuff means that she's really not interested in him.

Understanding of Expressions

Unable to recognize linguistic nuances, people with autism tend to take words literally and often believe everything they are told. This tendency, combined with blindness to social cues, can cause social disasters. A person with autism might ask an overweight woman why she is "so fat" or a bald man why is head is so "shiny." They often do not get jokes or understand lying and deceit. This problem can lead to obvious difficulties. I once worked with a teen with autism in a juvenile prison in Pennsylvania. This young man was arrested with a number of other teens after having done exactly what a "friend" told him to do. The young man was just following his friend's directions, so to speak, and did not realize that what he was asked to do was illegal—until the police arrested them.

The Autism Spectrum

In describing the manifestations of autism, I have used many qualifying words such as *frequently*, *often*, *sometimes*, and *might*. That's because it's hard to generalize characteristics of autism. As noted earlier, autism is diagnosed by observing behavior, but the observed behaviors vary tremendously from person to person. Having worked with thousands of people with autism, I have found that no two individuals who have autism seem to be alike. Although each may have similar types of impairments, no two individuals are the same.

As with all of us, weaknesses are often accompanied by strengths. A child's measured intellectual abilities may be low, but she may have relatively strong language. A boy might have fairly good social skills but also engage in severe stimming. It is important to carefully observe children with autism and try to assume nothing. The goal is always to build on a child's gifts.

I account for the variability of symptoms by speaking of autism as a spectrum disorder. At one end of the spectrum is what used to be referred to as Asperger syndrome. This is a high-functioning form of autism in which the individual did not appear to have problems with early language development and did not show the cognitive deficits that others with autism seemed to have. Yet, they did exhibit other problems associated with autism, including poor social skills, repetitive behaviors, attachment to routines and rituals, stimming, and avoiding eye contact. It should also be understood that even today, many children with higher-functioning forms of autism aren't diagnosed for many years, in part, because their language and intellectual development appear to be typical and their other symptoms are misunderstood. With the introduction of the *Diagnostic and Statistical Manual of Mental Disorders,*

Fifth Edition (DSM-5), Asperger syndrome was merged into the global Autism-Spectrum Disorder category and is no longer considered a free-standing diagnosis. That being said, many people, even in the medical field, still reference the term *Asperger's*.

What Autism Is *Not*

It's important to be clear about what autism is *not*. As noted earlier, autism is not considered a psychiatric disorder or a mental illness. Psychiatric disorders are clinically significant patterns or syndromes rooted in an individual's life situation, brain chemistry, or other causes. The symptoms of psychiatric disorders usually change over time. They can usually be treated. By contrast, autism is a developmental disorder that is lifelong and relatively static; symptoms and behaviors are managed, not cured.

Autism is not a phase that will pass. The neurological impairments present at birth will always be present. They will manifest differently as a person grows older, and they can often be managed, but they will not change substantially. Teachers can and need to help children with autism work around and manage some of these impairments, but they can't help them to "get better." Even those who are very bright might return to stimming in times of sickness, grief, or severe stress.

Sebastian was a man of twenty-four when his mother came to my office. At the time, Sebastian was working in a competitive job, was quite independent, and was living on his own. Tearfully his mother approached me and asked me if I thought Sebastian was "regressing." She stated that he had begun "stimming" again, flapping his hands, something he hadn't done since he was two years of age. When I eventually asked about the onset of the "flapping" behaviors, Sebastian's mother reported that it seemed to start around the time of his father's death. It was then we realized that Sebastian didn't know how to manage the emotion surrounding his father's passing, how to understand or respond to the death of someone so important in his life. As Sebastian was a very high-functioning young man, we began some supportive cognitive behavioral therapy, including methods of replacing hand-flapping behaviors with writing down happy thoughts and memories of activities that he and his father did together. He would later review these with his mother and at times when he was feeling upset. The hand-flapping behavior began fading within a few weeks and eventually was extinguished.

An important note: Autism is not caused by deficient child-rearing, stress in the home, or other psychological factors in the child's environment. It is not caused by evil spirits. It is not God's punishment for the parents' sins. Autism can occur in any family. The condition is found in all societies and in all racial and ethnic groups.

For people with autism, stimming and other unusual behaviors associated with autism are not intentional. They are not hostile acts meant to disrupt groups, or stratagems to get out of class. They are forms of communication or reactions to excitement, stress, and confusion caused by the faulty processing of sensory input. There's nothing about it that one should take personally.

Summary

- Autism is a neurodevelopmental disorder that can be observed in a child usually around the age of two or three. It is a disorder that at present can't be cured. However, many of the symptoms or behaviors associated with it can be *managed*. While it is not a psychiatric disorder, for some individuals psychotropic medications can be effective in easing some of the symptoms associated with their autism spectrum disorder.
- In order to receive a diagnosis of an autism spectrum disorder, a young child's symptoms must meet a certain number of criteria, and they must be present as an array or system of delays or

impairments. These may include problems with the functional use of language; delays or regression in age-appropriate communication milestones, such as difficulties with socialization (particularly with peers); and repetitive behaviors. All of these conditions must be present (whether the child's parents recognize them for what they are or not) while the child is still a toddler. If these symptoms appear at a later age, they may suggest different disorders.

- A person with autism may have lower intelligence quotients and may not be able to talk, while another can be very intelligent and could qualify for gifted education. Autism tends to interfere with a person's ability to process information, often making problem solving slower than what we might consider normal.
- When dealing with a child with autism, we need to be sensitive, patient, and compassionate. A teacher, for instance, needs to recognize that a child with autism might not know how to ask a question in a conventional manner or be able to define a word that has more than one meaning. When homework is given, the teacher needs to ensure that the student with autism knows the process to complete the homework before it is assigned. Further, it is important, due to concepts like *Theory of Mind*, that the teacher checks for understanding. Assumptions must also be kept to a minimum—a teacher should never assume that a lack of questioning means that a child understands a given idea or concept.
- Finally, a teacher needs to recognize that students with autism often have splinter skills—very good skills in one subject compared to another. Most students with autism are concrete learners and, unfortunately, have difficulty generalizing what they learn from one concept to a similar one.

3

Rules Are Rules

The need for order, structure, and predictability is crucial for children with autism. This is why schools, Catholic schools in particular, where children wear uniforms or specific types of clothing and have clear, unchanging daily structures are so sought after. Knowing what is coming next and limiting surprises often help a child with autism to thrive. When sudden change occurs, the child will likely have a difficult time. Worry ensues, causing the child to lash out or retreat. The following are examples of why structure and rules are so crucial for a child with autism to succeed in day-to-day school life.

The Substitute Teacher

Mark, our student who was introduced at the beginning of this book, is finally getting into a routine at school. For weeks, every day was pretty predictable, with the same schedule. Gradually, Mark understood that each day began with sitting at his desk while the teacher took attendance. This was followed by the Pledge of Allegiance, which was followed by a review of the daily calendar at the start of circle time. In fact, by the end of September, all was going so well that his teacher decided that it was safe for her to go to her doctor for a small elective surgery that she couldn't have done before the start of the semester. She carefully informed the class in advance that she would be away for the day and even put it on the class calendar so that everyone knew a week in advance which day would be affected. What could go wrong? Well, the poor substitute teacher didn't understand the concept of rules and routines for children with autism, that nothing could be changed or altered in the schedule. She took attendance and the students recited the Pledge of Allegiance, but she skipped the review, going straight to circle time. Mark was not happy.

Mark told her she was "doing it wrong." But he couldn't be more specific than that. Frustrated, he became more upset, repeating that the substitute was doing it wrong. The more the poor teacher tried to regain control of the classroom, the more upset Mark became. He ended up in a full meltdown with screaming and crying. He even knocked his chair over and was so upset that the substitute teacher ended up having to call the principal for help. Mark ended up going home before midmorning, all because the routine was mistakenly altered, throwing off his entire day.

Mark needs to know the *order of things* because he has difficulty anticipating events and responding to change. It's an *executive functioning process*, where a fixed routine frees him up to worry only about new things or surprises. However, when a set structure is changed, for example, when a substitute teacher inadvertently changes a scheduled event, or when a school assembly changes the order or duration of classes, a child with autism can go into panic mode.

Mark, like many students with autism, has trouble organizing things. Children with autism can't help it. Neurologically, most children simply need to learn how to manage challenges—with a new teacher, there is a new order to how things are done. For children with autism, however, their brains are like a room full of papers and books, which are all exciting things that they want to experience at the same time. This can become overwhelming without some way to sort through it all. So, they depend upon structure and order, and all of these great things (a new teacher, an assembly, unexpected or unstructured classroom activities or a special event) mix up that structure and order of a typical day for the child with autism. This causes confusion and discomfort that in many cases leads to meltdowns, particularly in younger children with autism.

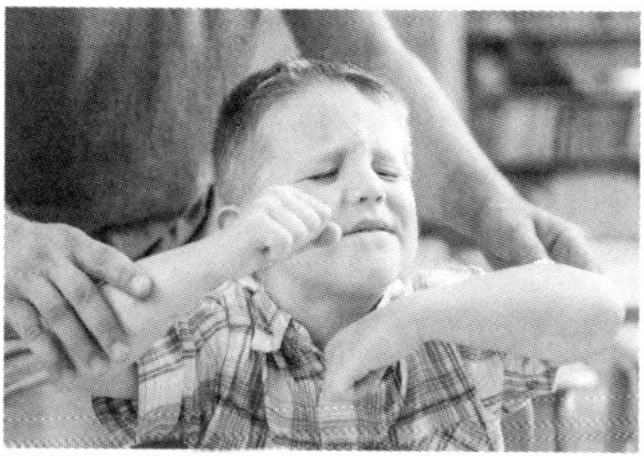

As stated in chapter 2, Executive function is generally considered to be the cognitive ability to control and regulate certain behaviors, such as the ability to recognize how to begin or interrupt certain actions. Executive function allows one to anticipate an outcome and to adapt a routine to changing situations. The ability to form concepts and think abstractly are often considered components of executive function, including the ability to remember things as well as the order of events and sequences.

Individuals with *executive function deficits*, whether due to a developmental delay, a disorder, or some sort of neurologic injury, (even individuals who have very high intelligence quotients), experience interference in their ability to perform some types of cognitive processes, including immediate recall, long-term memory, organizing things, and planning.

Particularly with younger children, *routines* are very important to help decrease anxieties about what is to come next. Therefore, behaviors in school, after the first month, are often much better than at home because of the predictability of events in each school day. For example, a child may hate mathematics but knows that math is confined to a specific school period each day. The child then learns, so to speak, how to isolate and *manage* through that difficult time, knowing that at the end of the period a different class will begin.

Problems can still arise in school when something special or unexpected takes place, such as a weather delay or another unanticipated event. The routine changes, and the child with autism can't remember what would come next. As a result, like during the first month of school, the child may panic, become flustered, shut down, or go into a meltdown.

When Rules Are Broken

When a teacher talks, students are to listen. Everything a teacher says is, in effect, a "rule," and a child with autism "needs" rules to be enforced (if they are to be *real* rules). As such, every time a rule is broken or not adhered to, a response or consequence *is required* on the part of the teacher or principal. Children with autism can be very tolerant of teachers, for they understand that it isn't possible for a teacher to see everything in a classroom. However, students with autism can take it upon themselves to "tell the teacher" about every infraction of a rule, or so it may seem. Many children with autism are like behavior police, always pointing out any infraction that deviates from the norm. After a while, this can be very tedious for the teacher. Moreover, this can hurt the child by making it difficult to make or keep friends. He or she is often labeled a tattletale by fellow students. When another child does not raise his hand to talk in the classroom or cuts into line or colors outside the boxes, it can greatly disturb the child with autism. The student with autism will attempt to follow all directions to the letter and, in some cases, may attempt to provide a "perfect" response even on a routine assignment. Subsequently, the student may be disappointed when the teacher does not praise him or her for the extraordinary effort he or she put into an assignment.

Summary

There are many "rules" in schools. This chapter addressed some of the important early rules to which teachers of young students with autism might need to attend. It is important to remember that each time the teacher (or caregiver) does something new, a child with autism will often take that behavior as the "right" or "correct" way for something to be done, *and* each time the rule is not done *correctly* (the way he or she first observed it), it is likely that the child with autism will tell you about it. As a result, it is important for a teacher who has a child or children with autism in his or her class to plan in advance how a new lesson is to be taught and studied. If the subject happens to be something the child with autism likes, can he or she have a part in teaching it? If the method of teaching is different, it might be important to explain the new method to the class before beginning the lesson. Further, it might be helpful to put a visual schedule outlining the lesson on the white board so the class can see the progression of the lesson. Finally, with lessons on new subjects, it might be important to provide the opportunity for homework to be done, or at least started, before the student goes home for the day.

4

What's in a Word? The Need for Functional Communication

Many children with autism appear shy when they first meet someone new, especially an adult like a doctor or a new teacher. Brian was one of those children. Early in the school year he would quietly sit at his desk, never raising his hand to respond to any of the teacher's questions. Still, based on his responses on class quizzes and tests, it seemed that he understood much of what was being taught in his language arts class. But as he never looked toward the teacher and never talked in class, it was difficult for his teacher to tell what he understood and what he didn't. When called upon during a lesson, typically Brian would shake his head in response to a question or would simply look down until the teacher spoke to someone else.

As the first month of the fall semester was coming to an end, Brian had still not uttered a word in class. He did speak with his brother at lunch and on the playground, and he stood near class peers at other times of the school day, but he rarely said a word when in the presence of his teacher.

Concerned and a little frustrated, Brian's teacher contacted his parents and asked to meet with them. She explained that from an academic perspective, Brian was doing well in school, but it was difficult to tell if he was being challenged too much, if he was bored, or if he was scared in class. The teacher went on to say that Brian did not clearly show any outward sign of his emotions or feelings and that he rarely looked at the teacher.

In turn, Brian's parents shared that he had an amazing memory and that he loved sports, especially professional sports. They mentioned that Brian could identify most of the players on any of the professional football teams. Furthermore, he could tell you the statistics of individual players and was pretty good at predicting, based on past individual game performance, which teams were likely to win on any given weekend.

Brian's teacher then had an idea. She asked the parents if she could conduct a lesson on basic elementary probability using Brian's ability to predict weekly football team winners. That is, the teacher suggested that each Thursday afternoon, the upcoming professional football matchups would be listed on the whiteboard. She would then ask the class to predict who would win each contest.

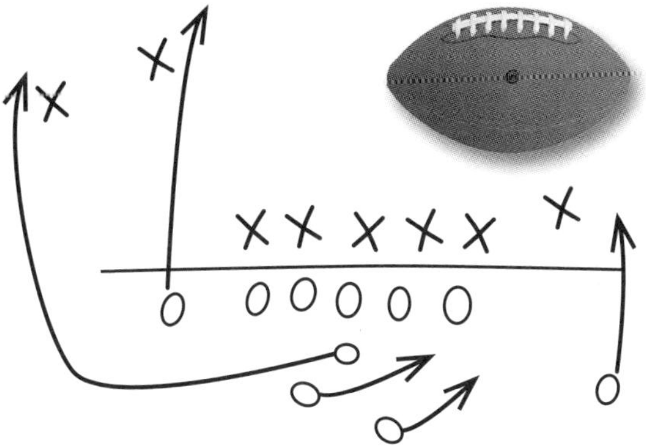

The parents approved of the idea, and the teacher put her plan into place. It worked. As football was a special interest of Brian's, he immediately looked toward the teacher as she described the lesson. She stated that the student who had picked the highest percentage of winners for the past weekend would then be asked to "predict" winning teams for the next weekend, and the rest of the class could vote to either agree or disagree. On the following Monday, the class met, and not surprisingly, Brian predicted eleven of the thirteen winners. He had the highest percentage of accuracy picking winners in the class. The teacher then asked Brian to look at the next week's football match-ups, and by Thursday afternoon, to "predict" winners for the next weekend. The rest of the class voted to agree or disagree with Brian. The results of this simple lesson were incredible, not only because Brian seemed to predict 85 percent of the winners each week but also because most of Brian's classmates came up to him at various times of the week to talk football. This seemed to boost Brian's self-confidence and elevated his engagement with his fellow students. He became, in effect, a classroom expert on professional football. Consequently, the teacher found that Brian began speaking during some of his other classes during the day as well. Brian's classmates viewed his special interest in football as highly valuable and asked his opinion about that topic often. As a result, Brian began talking more and even began asking some questions in classes taught by the teacher who created this lesson. This simple lesson didn't make Brian outgoing in school, but it clearly helped create an atmosphere where he felt safe. This led to his increased participation in class, which was heavily reinforced with positive comments by both his teacher and most of his classmates.

Acquiring functional communication skills is one of the most critical needs for children and teens with autism. Successfully communicating one's needs, wants, and interests to caregivers (including teachers) is essential to many aspects of cognitive and social development.

As described in the case of Antonio (in chapter 2), sometimes children with autism take a long time to understand what is being said to or asked of them. When Antonio entered high school (and was talking in full sentences), it would often take as long as sixty seconds before he could respond to a question. Ironically, when given that much time to respond to questions, Antonio typically provided responses that were spot on. However, although he wanted to participate in class, the discussions and lessons often moved too fast for him. Antonio lagged behind because of the length of time it would take for him to formulate a response to a question posed during regular class time. This latency in responding to questions, despite Antonio's ability to provide correct and thought-out answers, was problematic for his teachers. How can a teacher conduct a lesson when one or more of her students requires so much time to answer a single question? After meetings with Antonio, his parents, his school principal, and two of his teachers, the school agreed to a one-on-one teaching situation for him. In the classes where Antonio's response time did not affect the class (math, art, and library science), he remained in the typical class environment. In others, where he would benefit from extra time, he worked individually with a teacher.

Sometimes latency or delay in responding to questions isn't the only challenge teachers face in their classroom with children who have autism. Nancy, a very talkative second-grade student, would often raise her hand to provide an answer to a posed question. However, many times Nancy's responses didn't seem to be related to her teacher's question. For example, Nancy's teacher would ask the class what the main theme of the story was in the previous night's homework assignment. Nancy's hand quickly went up. Even before being called upon, Nancy began talking about how she sat down to do her homework and how her older brother got into trouble at home for not doing one of his chores. Even when directed back to the homework assignment by her teacher, Nancy couldn't focus on the question at hand. She became distracted by a picture hanging on the classroom wall near her desk and began talking about how she liked the picture. She never did talk about the homework assignment. In this case, Nancy was looking for positive reinforcement from her teacher by simply talking. The young girl enjoyed speaking but was easily distracted by the things she experienced in her life.

Functional communication, then, means both understanding what is being asked and being able to provide a response related to the question posed. It also includes being able to articulate wants and desires. Nancy's teacher eventually began asking her specific yes or no questions about the question posed that was related to her homework assignment as a way to keep her on track. This worked like a charm to keep her responses focused.

Developmental Issues

Typically, children connect and bond with their parents and caregivers very early in their lives. Children without auditory-processing impairments learn and then recognize that their parents make certain sounds. They also learn that making and responding to certain sounds mean something. As children grow, the sounds they hear and make eventually become words. Often children are able to say their first recognizable words on or before their first birthday and are able to put those words together to form small phrases and sentences by eighteen months of age. Sometimes children are delayed in recognizing the association between certain sounds and meeting their needs. This may be related to cognitive issues, such as delays in speech development, language acquisition, and/or functional communication, or other global developmental delays, including autism. In some instances, children may begin developing verbal language and use basic words or short phrases to communicate. Then, for reasons we don't fully understand, these children will lose that ability, often before their second birthday. This is not uncommon among children with autism.

With most children who have been identified as having an autism spectrum disorder, language, when it is present, is often direct, literal, and functional. Nuance in speech is often deficient. These children often do not understand when a word or phrase might have more than one meaning. They often don't understand the use of subtle variations in tone or changes in delivery, which might change the meaning of a word or phrase. As a result, they might miss the intent or misinterpret the meaning of a given communication.

Here's a case in point: Elizabeth was a fifth-grade student in a very active classroom. Her teacher struggled at times keeping order and structure to his lessons because of the many active students in the class. He often had class meetings where he would state clearly and concisely what the rules were and what the consequences would be for breaking them. Even though Elizabeth was one of the students who never seemed to break the rules, she would frequently tell her parents upon arrival at home from school that her teacher had "yelled at her" in school that day. It wasn't until the first parent-teacher meeting that the teacher was made aware of Elizabeth's understanding of the teacher's statements to the class. The teacher explained to the parents that Elizabeth wasn't in fact the target of those statements, as she was one of the students who consistently followed the rules. Rather, the review of the rules was addressed to the entire class as a way of benchmarking a certain level of order. Elizabeth interpreted the teacher's words personally and literally, as if they were directed specifically to her, and as a result she would go home and report that the teacher yelled at her.

Children and teens with autism often struggle with changes in the tone of speech of a teacher or parent. This could be due in part to a certain level of self-centeredness, which leads to a belief by the individual with autism that he or she is the central focus of the world, a concept drawn from the *Theory of Mind.* In this context, they will take a teacher's general statements to an entire classroom personally, as if the words were directed exclusively to them. When possible, it is important for the teacher to be specific about to whom statements are directed when addressing the class about desired or undesired behaviors, and who is an example of someone behaving appropriately.

As noted earlier, students with autism struggle when words or phrases have more than one meaning. Most of these words or concepts need to be taught individually or directly to a child with autism, unlike their neurotypical peers, who seem to process multiple meanings more quickly. In a concrete sense, a child with autism can learn, for example, that two plus two equals four but still needs to be taught that three plus one or four plus zero also equal four. When words have more than one meaning, or when there is more than one method for solving a problem, the child with autism can become anxious, confused, and upset. This literal interpretation of language and understanding of rules or mathematical principles is in part why children with autism are often bullied or taken advantage of by peers. They often become easy targets for bullies who may use their literalism against them.

If a child has had a good language evaluation (something that most children with autism need to have conducted periodically as they grow older), a teacher reviewing such a report could learn a great deal about how a child understands language and how the child learns. Typically, language evaluations are conducted by a licensed and certified speech-language pathologist (indicated with "CCC-SLP" after their name). In a language evaluation, a teacher can learn how a child hears or comprehends what is said to him or her (auditory comprehension or receptive language). Teachers can also detect if a child has difficulty expressing thoughts or feelings (expressive language skills) as well as learn to understand a child's ability to use words, sentences, and connected discourse (telling stories, retelling events).

Good language evaluations often provide examples of how to work on cultivating and improving language skills. This is particularly the case when looking at pragmatic language skills, which are used in relating socially to one's peers. The use of language in social communication, including the ability to use nonverbal communication and recognize it in others will often help the teacher better recognize the nature of a child's difficulty when interacting with other children. A teacher can model correct use of language between two students so that the child with autism has an example of what to do differently. In this way, a child with autism can learn pragmatic language skills while doing typical schoolwork in the classroom, interacting on the playground, or eating in the cafeteria.

Although not common in typical Catholic school classrooms, some children with autism may arrive to school with augmentative communication devices (speech-generating devices or picture-exchange systems). It is important in such instances that the teacher has a working knowledge of how the device operates and how it is to be used by the specific student. It is also important to ask the child's parents how they use the device at home.

In a personal communication with the author about reviewing a language-evaluation report, Lori J. Marra, MA, CCC-SLP writes, "I think a teacher should be able to gather what specific language areas (listening, reading, expression, and writing) will affect academics." This report can provide a teacher with valuable information about how an individual student understands language. For example, a child with language-comprehension (receptive language) deficits may have difficulty with listening comprehension or following classroom directions as well as trouble with reading comprehension. Children with autism are typically good decoders and have good reading fluency scores but have difficulty deducing meaning in what they have read because of language comprehension problems. Many times, children with autism have a diagnosis that includes an expressive language problem, which can take two forms, oral or written. Oral expression problems include word finding or language organization difficulties. Children with these language deficits can't describe steps in a familiar task, organize a story, or retell or explain something they themselves understand.

Written expression problems include disorganized thoughts and the sole use of a very basic sentence structure. Sometimes higher-level language skill deficits, like difficulty in understanding inferences, may be reported. These deficits will affect reading comprehension and social communication and conversations.

When looking at test results and diagnosis, a teacher will be provided with specific recommendations for strategies, supports, or accommodations that will help that child. For example, children who have autism are often slow processors of information and may need additional time to complete a task or may need visual supports such as pictures, graphic organizers, or word banks.

Summary

When children with autism are able to effectively communicate their needs, they are, and feel, better understood. They can relax, move forward in learning, and advance socially and intellectually in the classroom. When children feel understood, they are more likely to use the intellectual gifts that God has given them and often do so in surprising and exceptional ways.

When a teacher understands and knows his or her student (with autism) really well, that child is likely to be better understood and will likely achieve better results in the classroom. Ultimately, the student will most likely be happier, knowing he or she is understood and doing well in class. In order to understand a student with autism, it is important that a teacher take advantage of the information that is available about the child; whether it is information provided by the child's parents, by other teachers, or through clinical evaluations and assessments—the key is to find those documents and to use the information in them to understand and respond every time a student with autism does something unexpected. It is important to remember that even though a child with autism may be a very bright individual, he or she may be quite literal in learning new things. This often requires step-by-step instructions to help the child to understand principles and excel. Taking time to get to know your student with autism from the beginning will yield remarkable dividends at the end.

5

Using Preferred Interests When Teaching Students with Autism

Early in my career, I made the mistake of asking a child to bring in one of her preferred interests, which she did. Be careful what you ask for. . . . When Sofia arrived at our next appointment, sitting between our two chairs in my office was a very complicated array of parts from a disassembled radio-controlled model car. I have no idea how she got it and all the separate parts into my office, but Sofia was beyond excited to share her prized possession with me and show me how it worked.

Do preferred interests help a teacher, or are they another problem for a teacher to address? This chapter will focus on emerging best practices to use in typical classrooms, including those that can use a personal focused interest of a child with autism to enhance learning.

What Is a Preferred Interest?

A preferred interest (sometimes referred to as a *restricted* or *focused* interest) is usually an object, subject, or idea of great personal value and focus for a child with autism. Many young children like trains, notably Thomas the Tank Engine, from the popular book and TV series. A child who seems unable to talk about anything else can sometimes burst with enthusiasm and share a series of details about Thomas, Percy, James, or any of the other characters on the imaginary Island of Sodor. This is, of course, something positive. But sometimes the child's interest can become so intense that it may interfere with school lessons and general learning.

I once worked with a nine-year-old named Lucas. He had a preferred interest in the Civil War. His interest was so developed that he could not only correctly identify the various generals and other officers who took part in the war but also name numerous battles, where they took place, and discuss quite freely what happened in those conflicts. This brought the boy great joy. His interest, however, could be triggered by unrelated references in class: for example, money. In a math lesson about coins, Lucas's teacher held up a penny and asked whose face was on it? Lucas shouted out, "Abraham Lincoln!" and then he began talking about the Civil War. Lincoln was, as we all know, President of the United States during that war. Lucas was so excited by the connection that it was hard to direct him back to the math lesson at hand. In this instance, Lucas's preferred interest in anything related to the Civil War interfered with his own learning as well as the class's math lesson.

However, knowing a child's preferred interest and using it as a part of a lesson can make a dramatic difference in class participation for a child with autism. If there is a way to incorporate a child's preferred interest in your lesson, the child can feel included and important. She can be held to be an "expert" on the subject. In Lucas's case, when Lucas was asked a question related to a specific general or another element of the Civil War, he would begin talking in intricate detail about the topic, so much so that he would not stop talking until redirected.

This type of preferred, or focused, interest may have started with some benign activity, such as collecting an object related to that interest and having one of his parents or grandparents praise him through a smile or other positive gesture. This interest may have been reinforced over time. Of course, this is just one example. A preferred interest may develop in many ways, but what we do know is that when a child locks on to something that stimulates his creativity and imagination, his passion for the idea or thing can increase with intensity over days, weeks, months, and years.

A teacher needs to decide whether to use or not use the preferred interests of a child with autism in his or her day-to-day lessons. There are, of course, pros and cons. On the one hand, one method of including the child with autism in a typical or mainstream classroom is to put a focus on his or her preferred interest in a lesson, thereby keeping the child focused on what the teacher is presenting. On the other hand, a teacher may risk losing the interest and focus of other students in the classroom by spending too much time on the preferred interest of the child with autism. In addition, the child with autism may focus only on the preferred interest and not attend to the lesson. The teacher must weigh all options. But it is important to remember that a child's preferred interests can be viewed as expressions of his or her personal gifts or skill sets. Sharing these interests with similar aged peers in his or her classroom is very prestigious and may lead to increased social communication with these same peers, particularly when they are given the responsibility of leading a part of a class lesson.

Let's get back to Lucas's story. Lucas's preferred interests were problematic in several areas. First, he had trouble making and keeping friends. Lucas was typically seen as a quiet child—until something triggered his preferred interest. Then he would begin talking and would continue, even when his classmates lost interest. When a peer began walking away after growing bored with the topic, Lucas would continue talking about the subject while following the peer. Second, it became a dilemma for the teacher who was trying to engage Lucas in classroom discussions related to topics that did not interest him. The teacher attempted to engage Lucas by asking him to talk about a specific Civil War battle, only to have to abruptly stop him after a lengthy and detailed monologue, which most of the other students couldn't or didn't follow. Lucas lacked both the social cues to recognize when others were not as interested in something as he was, as well as when they might be bored or when the topic needed to be changed. As a result, Lucas often sat by himself at lunch or was alone on the playground, as none of his fellow classmates shared these specific interests to the same degree he did.

Should Lucas's teacher restrict Lucas or prevent him from talking about his interest in the American Civil War? If not, how can the teacher manage *what* or *how much* Lucas has to say on a specific question related to this preferred interest? Setting a specific amount of time for something to be presented often provides a needed structure that children with autism may be unable to create themselves.

Ultimately, it is important to remember that an inclusive classroom is one where all learners have the opportunity to pursue and enhance their God-given gifts and experience a community of acceptance, respect of differences, and dignity for everyone. So it is important to strike a balance between one child's preferred interest and the needs of the entire class in learning the assigned material.

Using Preferred Interests

In using the preferred interest of a child with autism, teachers need to personalize the support of a child's interest while finding innovative ways to include the needs and interests of each other student in the classroom. Incorporating a child's preferred interest allows for the recognition of his or her potential strengths rather than highlights an apparent weakness. As preferred interests are objects or topics of great importance to the child, ignoring or denying the child an opportunity to talk about or demonstrate that interest might lead to a decrease in the child's self-confidence.

Take these cases to illustrate this point: Billy was a young teen who enjoyed writing short stories. The stories often included a hero in some sort of familiar adventure. Because he was somewhat shy, Billy had a hard time making friends. Yet, when given the chance to read one of his stories, he beamed with pride, thrilled to have the opportunity to express something that brought him so much happiness. Or take for example, Jordan, who loved to doodle. He, too, had a difficult time beginning conversations or interactions with his peers, except when he began doodling. His simple drawings were so good that his peers often asked him to sketch objects for them. Jordan's history teacher, recognizing his strength in sketching, asked if he would be willing to "sketch out" a historical scene to help the teacher illustrate to the class what it may have looked like at that time in history. Jordan literally jumped at the chance!

In both instances, it was important for Billy and Jordan to be included in the class lesson in meaningful and positive ways. Involving them in the lesson not only increased their self-esteem but also benefited everyone else in the classroom, who got to learn new topics from different points of view. Conversely, if either of the teachers had chosen to ignore or not use Billy's or Jordan's skills in their lessons, he or she may have denied them the opportunity to be meaningfully engaged with their classmates. Sometimes ignoring a child's gifts in class and focusing on their perceived deficits puts a child at risk for depression and academic failure. So it is important to find ways to build and incorporate the strengths of a child with autism into lessons to reinforce their abilities and increase their engagement with their peers.

Including a child's preferred interest is both reinforcing and intrinsically motivating to the student with autism. Including preferred interests can help some children with autism keep their interest on a lesson and improve their performance while decreasing other possible disruptive behaviors. At Our Lady of Grace Catholic School in Pittsburgh, I recommended to a teacher that she consider "rewarding" her second-grade child, who had a high-functioning form of autism, with a set of flash cards containing vocabulary words in a second language (in this case, Spanish) when she knew the child clearly understood his mathematics review lesson. In this way, the child was highly motivated to please the teacher while at the same time the teacher's learning plan for him was enriched through a new reward and academic task, which was learning a second language.

Additionally, when providing an opportunity for a child with autism to express or show off a preferred interest, they often have a heightened sense of self-esteem and at times may speak more confidently and fluidly. Fluency in expressed language seems to be present more often when the child is conversing on a preferred interest. Furthermore, it often includes a wider range of vocabulary and improved conversational skills.

Using preferred interests can also support other tasks, like fine motor skills. Handwriting, cutting paper, and picking up objects can be a problem for many children with autism. I have found that when engaged in regular (at least weekly) occupational therapy sessions, combined with using a preferred interest, the handwriting of many children with autism can become more legible. However, within a month after ending that particular therapy, it seemed that the handwriting of the children with autism with whom I worked often returned to pre-therapy levels. Writing on a preferred interest did seem to increase the child's confidence, nevertheless.

Summary

Incorporating the preferred interest of a child with autism into a teacher's daily academic lessons by drawing something related to the subject being covered or reading a personal story for example, can increase the child's academic performance and may even keep the child focused longer on other subjects. This can work only when the teacher is aware of and can meaningfully incorporate the child's preferred interest into his or her lessons, as noted in the cases of Billy and Jordan. Discouraging or preventing focus on a child's preferred interest can lead to frustration and, at times, meltdowns because of the child's inability to fully express his or her feelings or needs.

Including preferred interests in lessons, social groups, and leisure activities should be encouraged. These opportunities bring the child's areas of interest and expertise into the classroom, which in turn, brings the attention of the child with autism into the classroom as well. When a teacher is unsuccessful in engaging the child, he or she may ultimately fail to activate the child's passion for learning. Including a preferred interest in some capacity of the school day in a sensitive and informed way will best support the child and bring out his or her learning potentials.

6

A Word on Behavior Management

When it comes to children with autism, most of the time behaviors are a form of communication. Each behavior can have a specific meaning. Unfortunately, we just don't always know at the time the behavior is displayed what its meaning is. What is important to know is that from an early age, children with autism associate certain behaviors as ways to get what they need and, thus, perform them when they need something. For example, I began working with Liza when she was seven years old. She was a bright girl who could clearly communicate to her parents and teachers the proper way to behave when angry or upset. Yet more often than not, Liza would punch her sister, Mary, when she was angry or upset and needed her mother's attention. Hitting Mary became so frequent that her parents were convinced that Liza had a severe behavior problem, maybe even a conduct disorder. In other words, they thought she had an antisocial behavior problem. At times they just thought that she was being oppositional on purpose. Interestingly, after striking her sister, Liza appeared genuinely remorseful and upset with herself for having hurt her sister. Still, when she was angry, Liza didn't know what else to do.

As I began working with Liza, I learned that when she was younger, she connected striking or pushing her sister to getting her mother's attention. That is, she *learned* that she could get her mother's attention more quickly by hitting Mary than by *asking* for her mother. As Liza got older, she learned that the best way to get Mom's attention was to do something aggressive to Mary, and although she may not have been angry or upset with Mary, this was the rule, so to speak, to get Mom's attention. As Liza grew older, she realized that she didn't always want to hit Mary, but she "didn't know" another way to get her mother's attention (despite being able to tell me numerous other ways that did not involve aggression toward her sister). After working with her for a short time, I did not believe that Liza had a conduct disorder or that she was being oppositional. Rather, in a time of need or at the peak of anger she always did what she did in that situation the time before: She hit Mary and was "rewarded" each time (her behavior was reinforced) by getting her mother's attention, even though it was typically negative attention.

Liza did not have a *replacement behavior* that was functional or that she had *practiced* as an alternative to hitting her sister when she wanted her mother's attention. When I spoke to Liza's parents, we discussed possible replacement behaviors that Liza could use instead of hitting Mary when Liza wanted to ask her mother for something. In this case, we began using the word *red* and proceeded to *role play* and *practice* the replacement behavior with Liza, her sister, and her mother. In effect, we began playing a game. For her part, Liza's mother made the conscious commitment to look out for and recognize the new signal or behavior, that is, she listened for the word *red*. Liza knew that she was not supposed to hit her sister and had subsequently practiced this replacement behavior and wanted to please her mother. The next time Liza became upset and wanted her mother, she yelled, "Red!" Liza's mother would then take that as a cue to respond to her daughter, knowing that she needed her attention. It seemed that from that point forward the old behavior of hitting her sister to get her mother's attention began fading. Liza was getting what she wanted by "pleasing" her mother, by using the replacement behavior when she wanted her mother instead of hitting her sister. Liza and her mother continued in this fashion, and although Liza will still hit her sister, it's no longer to get her mother's attention. Now, it's because she is angry at her sister, a problem requiring a different type of *replacement behavior*.

Many children with autism *do not know what to do* when they don't understand something a teacher is saying. Sometimes they just get bored, and they find it difficult to follow a lesson. As in any classroom, a student may ask a question or may not be ready to move on to another topic. When this happens, children with autism may grow restless while waiting. As a result, some of them may fidget, get out of their chairs, or start tapping on their desks. They seem to need a form of expression to either tell the teacher they don't understand what is being presented or that they do in fact get it but also need something to do while the teacher helps other students. In any case, *the child with autism then needs a way to manage the time*. A simple replacement behavior can help so that a disruptive behavior (fidgeting or getting out of their chair) doesn't occur. This is something children with autism typically can't do or create on their own and therefore requires help from a teacher. One simple method that works with all students with autism is to have the children learn and practice raising their hand while holding up a card of some sort to indicate to the teacher that the student has something to say, is confused, or may need something else altogether.

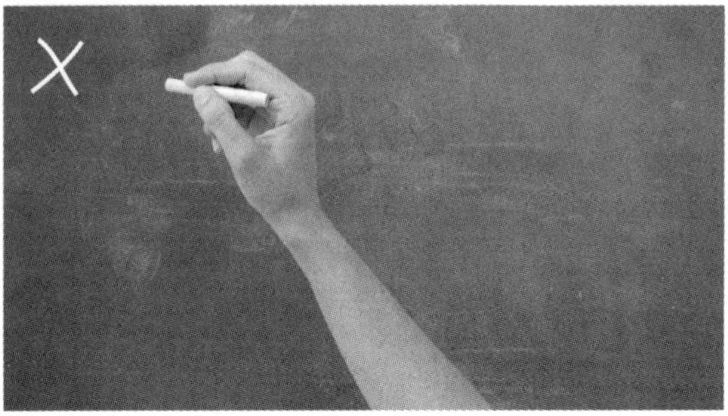

It is always good to be prepared with a method to help a child who has a lot of extra energy. In the case of a restless child, the teacher should meet with the child and his or her parents at the start of the school year. At this meeting, she can develop a few strategies for managing certain behaviors that are disruptive in the classroom, such as talking, calling out without being called on, or getting out of one's seat without being directed to do so. In the case of Dan, a bright and active third-grade student, it was agreed that each time he displayed one of the identified behaviors, such as calling out an answer before being called upon, the teacher would make an *X* on the top left-hand corner of the blackboard in the classroom. Dan initially knew that he was allowed no more than three *X* marks for each class period, and if he was successful in having three or fewer *X* marks in seven of his nine class periods, he would receive a reward. That is, at the end of the day his homeroom teacher would give him a certificate of achievement. Upon arriving home, Dan's parents would praise him and display the certificate by hanging it on the refrigerator. The certificate was something created on the teacher's classroom computer that she would update each day and print each of the days that Dan was successful. The next morning, the certificate would

be removed and placed in a special folder in Dan's father's desk at home for safe keeping, and the new day would then begin again. Eventually the disruptive behaviors were adjusted to allow for only one *X* per class period to obtain a certificate, which increased the difficulty for success but also acknowledged Dan's progress in controlling his behavior.

In Dan's situation, it was important to manage his disruptive classroom behaviors but not discourage his enthusiasm for learning. It was very important that Dan be successful in the new plan to manage his classroom behaviors, so the plan was initially made easy for him. As the plan developed, Dan "learned" that it was important to earn the certificate each day. Each time one of his teachers began reaching for the marker for the white board, Dan would stop what he was doing and become compliant with the plan. As time went on, he learned to control his behavior, so the risk of getting an *X* was eliminated, but he also had the chance to recover if he slipped up during one class period.

Of note, when using a plan like this, it's important that the child learn that one bad experience, a meltdown in one class or getting four *X*s in another class, didn't "ruin the day." That is, it didn't ruin his chances of bringing home the prized certificate for the day if he did well in seven of the eight other classes that day. In this way, when he moved to the next class or lesson, he knew that the white board would start out blank again, and he was able to "start over" in the new class period. He learned over time that one bad experience in the morning, didn't ruin the whole day.

Functional Behavioral Analysis

A Functional Behavioral Analysis (FBA) is typically created by a psychologist or a professional who is certified in Applied Behavioral Analysis (ABA). It provides information, guidance, and possible treatment recommendations for dealing with problematic behavior of a person at home and/or in school in order to change or manage the identified behavior. This is done by understanding the context of the behavior to determine its function, which is the desired outcome or purpose the behavior serves for a child with autism. Once a function can be determined, a more desirable behavior can be substituted to modify or replace the undesirable problematic behavior.

The process begins by looking at particular behaviors that come before a problematic behavior surfaces (see Figure 1). Then the professional will look at the problematic behavior itself and look at what happens as the result of the problematic behavior. In the case of a child who has autism, it is important to see how this disability affects behavior as well. Creating a simple ABC Chart can help analyze the behavior chain and its outcomes. An ABC Chart is a tool that is frequently used to better understand a given problematic behavior. *A* stands for Antecedent (what happens before), *B* is for Behavior (the action or reaction to the Antecedent), and *C* is for Consequence (what happens after, or the outcome of the Behavior).

Figure 1: Functional Assessment of Behavior

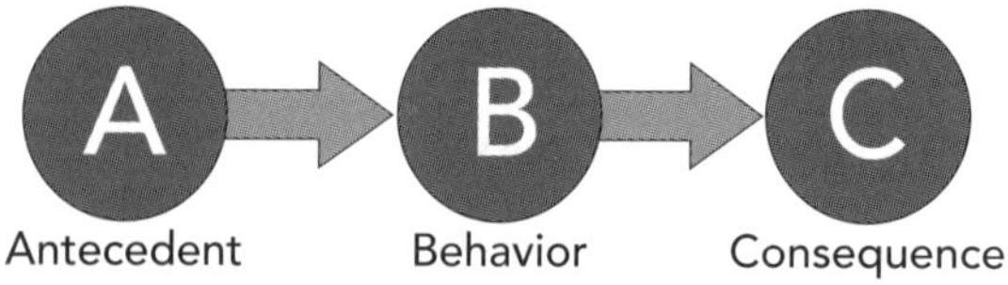

When a child displays a problematic behavior, the teacher tries to better understand the context of that behavior by looking at where and when the behavior happened and where and when that behavior does not seem to present itself. The teacher then looks at how often that behavior is occurring, who is around when it occurs (other students, teachers, and staff) and then looks at what happens both immediately before and right after the behavior happens. Once this information is known, the teacher may try to identify a more acceptable behavior to begin shaping the child's response to one that is more desired. Although this analysis of a child's behavior is typically done and reviewed by a psychologist or a behavior analyst, it isn't too complicated or difficult for a teacher to interpret and implement. With a little bit of direction and supervision, teachers tend to do a very good job of understanding the process and creating a good plan to manage problematic behaviors.

It is important to remember that when looking at a problematic behavior of a student with autism, the behavior might be a call for attention or used to remedy a sensory problem the student may be experiencing, such as a buzzing florescent light or a neighbor humming a song, which is distracting. The function might also be to express that the child doesn't understand something the teacher has said. With no better way to communicate her uncertainty, the child throws a tantrum. Or, perhaps the function of the behavior might be that the child doesn't want to do something, like take a test or a quiz. In this case, stimming, for example, can become a way of avoiding something the child finds too unpleasant. If behavior, whether it is stimming or some other behavior, is not addressed by the teacher, it could potentially develop into a meltdown when the activity it is aimed at avoiding or soothing is "too unpleasant" from the child's perspective.

As noted above, a recurring behavioral episode of the student with autism is often a *form of communication*. A child has learned that a certain behavior will get him what he or she needs. For example, saying, "Juice please," typically gets the child a glass of juice, or raising a hand in school lets the teacher know the student has a question. In the case of Antonio, mentioned in chapter 2, when the class discussion was moving too fast for him, he would begin to strike his head on his desk, which inevitably slowed the class discussion down. However, although Antonio's method was very *successful* (in that it slowed the classroom discussion), it wasn't the most *functional* way to get what he needed, since it could potentially hurt Antonio's head. We found that a healthier way for Antonio to tell us that we were moving too fast was for him to simply stand up. Each time Antonio stood during a class lesson, I stopped and asked him to tell me about the lesson we were doing. This would help me know where he was in his level of understanding of the lesson. In this way, Antonio successfully communicated that the lesson was moving too fast for him, but he expressed it in a way that did not involve him hurting his head. Typically, when this occurred, Antonio's summaries were accurate, up to a point, which gave me a place to begin my review or a clue that it was okay to carry on. By stopping the lesson, we allowed his processing to catch up, and the lesson then continued or picked up at the point of his understanding. Note that we were not able to use this method in each of Antonio's classes; he did require some one-on-one instruction for several specific classes.

By conducting an analysis of a child's behavior, a teacher can develop an understanding of what his or her student might need or want. It might give the teacher an idea of why a student is acting out. With the information gained from an analysis of the child's behavior, a teacher might then be able to modify what he or she is doing in class so that the student can better understand a lesson, while at the same time teaching the student better ways to get the teacher's attention. Please note, this is the same approach that a teacher might take with *any* child in his or her class with a problematic behavior, not just with a child with autism.

In the case of problematic behaviors with children who have autism, it is important to understand that most problematic behaviors are either "learned behaviors," which might need to be retaught in a different way, or methods of communicating a problem. Although the techniques used in conducting a Functional Behavioral Analysis are highly specialized, the methodology is straightforward. Depending on the relationship of a private Catholic school with the local public school, the services of a school psychologist or behavior analyst might be available to help support the creation of Functional Behavioral Analysis for a given student.

Visual Schedules

Simple behavioral charts and visual daily/weekly schedules posted in the classroom can be effective means of both informing and managing many typical behaviors in most classrooms. Children with autism will benefit greatly when they can see rules and schedules. The clarity that comes from consistent schedules, and consequences when rules are not followed, often frees up the child with autism to focus on less clear items in a school day, such as nonstructured play during recess and lunch, how to respond during an assembly, or how to act during weekly Mass.

	Monday	Tuesday	Wednesday	Thursday	Friday
8 am	Check Homework	Check Homework	Check Homework	Check Homework	Check Homework
9 am	Spelling	Writing	Music	Writing	Spelling
10 am	Math	Math	Art	Math	Math
11 am	Gym	Reading	Gym	Reading	Gym
12 Noon	Lunch	Lunch	Lunch	Lunch	Lunch

	Monday	Tuesday	Wednesday	Thursday	Friday
4 pm	Homework	Homework	Homework	Homework	Homework
5 pm	Play	Play	Play	Play	Play
6 pm	Dinner	Dinner	Dinner	Dinner	Dinner
7 pm	Chores	Chores	Chores	Chores	Chores
8 pm	Brush Teeth	Brush Teeth	Brush Teeth	Brush Teeth	Brush Teeth
8:30 pm	Bedtime	Bedtime	Bedtime	Bedtime	Bedtime

Partnering for Success

Remember that when working on behavioral issues in your classroom, it is critical to include the child's parents in the design of interventions, plans, and schedules. There are times that a child's parents may be managing a similar behavior at home, and in some cases the strategies used at home may be very effective for the classroom. In these instances, there is no need to reinvent a method to manage a specific problematic behavior if a successful method already exists.

Take the example of Jaime and the use of the white board on the home refrigerator. Jaime is a fourth-grade student with a lot of energy. When he is bored, he becomes restless and either fidgets or roams aimlessly about the room. In an attempt to deal with similar problems at home, his parents began using a small white board attached to their refrigerator with a magnet. When Jaime began engaging in an undesired behavior, such as picking up the television remote and surfing through channels when another family member was already watching something on the television, his parents would make a check mark on the white board. Jaime knows that if he has fewer than three marks on that board in an evening, he gets to pick a snack or sticker before bedtime. Recognizing the value of the white board at home, Jaime and his teacher agreed that she will use the same strategy at school for when Jaime is bored. If he has fewer than three marks by the end of the morning and again at the end of the day, he has the opportunity to earn a (limited) homework pass or the option to do another desired activity. By giving Jaime the opportunity to participate in a program that he already understands, he is more likely to succeed in his day-to-day activities at school.

Summary

Children with autism often communicate wishes and desires, happiness or sadness through their behaviors. When observing and/or responding to a meltdown, tantrum, or behavioral outburst of a student who has an autism spectrum disorder, it is important to remember that these behaviors are often a form of communication for that child. In many cases, the outburst is the result of the child either not having a replacement behavior to use or having learned that a certain (aberrant) behavior will lead to his or her getting what he or she wants or needs. Recognizing what the behavior actually means, its *function*, is the first step in better understanding the child, and what he or she might be needing at a particular time. In understanding the child and his or her behavior, a teacher can then often anticipate what that child might need or want before a meltdown or behavioral outburst occurs.

7

The Value of Peer Mentors

I learned many valuable, and often surprising, lessons about teaching children with autism while writing my first book, *How to Welcome, Include, and Catechize Children with Autism and Other Special Needs: A Parish-Based Approach*. I found, for example, that many neurotypical teens (teenagers without developmental disabilities) have a real passion for helping others, especially those with disabilities. Further, when given the responsibility of working one-on-one with a child who has a disabling condition, these individuals have good instincts and solid work ethics. Take Nicholas for example. His peer, Josh, had a high-functioning form of autism and a pretty good command of language. Sometimes Josh would start talking about random topics during the group part of our class, and Nicholas, who was sitting next to Josh, would lightly put his hand on Josh's arm. This light touch would prompt Josh to immediately shift his focus to me as I gave the week's reflection. Nicholas and Josh grew close over time, and even though Nicholas was only seventeen and wasn't a special educator per se, he gained Josh's trust. As a result, Nicholas was able to help Josh to learn his lessons each week.

I learned that with the help of neurotypical teenagers serving as mentors, we were able to measurably demonstrate educational growth in children and teens with autism that were following our religious education program. Teen faith mentors provide both educational and, perhaps more important, social support for students with autism, helping them to learn in a safe and friendly environment. Children with autism learn in a firsthand way what is important to do and to talk about as a result of being with a teen mentor.

Instructional Time in Classrooms

Like many children, students with autism learn by the modeling of their peers, which they then imitate. This learning can be both good and bad. However, when a typical teen is intentionally paired with a child or another teen with autism, I have found that the mentor becomes *empowered*. Given the responsibility of helping a peer, these teens most often become good, safe Catholic role models for their mentees.

Mentors can help a child with a disability in two ways: academically and socially.

Academic Support

Most students with autism can typically learn better from near-aged peers than from an adult teacher or instructor *on some* lessons. These peer mentors, once they learn how to communicate with their students, are often able to convey information to a student with autism so that the essentials of a lesson are understood. In my experience, the students with autism seemed to learn materials faster and retain information longer when it came from their peer mentor.

I can remember formally meeting with Sean before his Confirmation, quizzing him on what it meant to be an adult in the church. Sean couldn't provide me with an immediate clear answer about what it meant to be a confirmed Catholic adult. However, when I asked him more specific questions about the sacraments, I was blown away by his answers. For example, when I asked what the gifts of the Holy Spirit were, not only did he quickly recite them, but he defined each as he spoke. He provided a simple but clear response to the question of who the Holy Spirit is and what is meant by the sacrament of initiation. Sean then surprised me by providing the answer on how *he would be different* after receiving the sacrament; that is, what it meant to be an adult in our church. I asked him how he knew all of this, and he responded that he and his mentor, Jack, developed their own study guide on "things to know about confirmation," which were taken from their weekly lessons. Each week, they added something new after they reviewed the entire list and then worked on the new lesson. Although there is more to being a confirmed adult in the Catholic Church than memorizing a list, this method became a foundation for understanding the sacrament for both Sean and Jack.

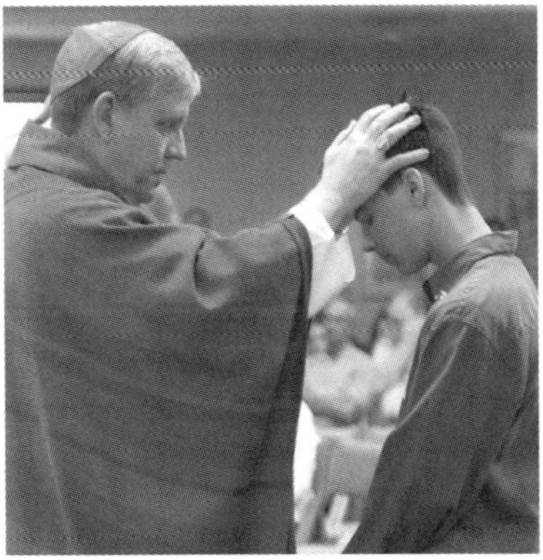

Peer mentors provide another layer of structure for children with autism. They can help with homework or assist children when they get lost in a lesson that moves too fast. Mentors can help keep children with autism focused on a task, worksheet, or test, often just by pointing to the student's paper. Later, the mentor may be able to alert the teacher to aspects of the lesson that the mentee may not have understood, which allows the teacher to help increase the student's understanding at a later time by focusing on those aspects.

Social Support

As noted earlier, a peer mentor often cues a student through subtle and sometimes nonverbal methods. This helps the child with autism understand what he or she *should or should not* do in numerous social situations.

For example, most teens with autism need to watch and observe a person or an activity before they know how to act in a new social situation. This was most evident to me on the evening I took a group of students with autism and their mentors to a professional hockey game. During the game, one of the teens with autism essentially sat and observed his teen mentor "have fun" in this new setting. That is to say, while at the hockey game, the teen with autism sat and watched how his peer mentor reacted when one team scored a goal. He also observed how his mentor reacted when the same team let up a goal, that is, with disappointment or sadness. Throughout the game, the teen with autism sat and did not appear to react when either team scored a goal. I asked him on three occasions if he was having a good time. He responded yes. But I was still skeptical. To my eyes it didn't look like he was having a good time at all. However, when that same teen attended a subsequent hockey game with his mentor, he appeared to react just as his mentor did, appropriately with happiness and excitement when the home team scored a goal and with disappointment when the home team gave up a goal. It became apparent to me that the teen with autism had needed to learn how to have fun in that new activity. Although I should have known it, people with autism often have to learn the rules for new situations, even when it comes to having fun at sporting events, birthday parties, or other special events.

Socially, due in part to the idea that the "world revolves around me," teens with autism often struggle in social situations. To these teens, everything that happens around them seems to occur because of them.

Further, as students with autism grow into adolescence, many do not know which of their peers (if any) they can trust, due in part to their having been teased or bullied. When formally paired with a teen mentor, children and teens with autism have someone they can trust and will watch and listen to their mentors. They will observe how they dress, how they talk with others, and how they act around their own peers. In effect, they are using the teen mentor as a *safe* guide or model for how to be and how to survive as a teenager.

My use of teen faith mentors in teaching children and teens with autism about God in faith-formation programs has been surprisingly successful. Many teen faith mentors are quick to learn the best type of language to use when communicating with their partners. Further, many faith mentors become experts in reading cues from their partners, especially when the students with autism become confused or bored by a lesson, which ultimately leads to shifting of attention. At those times, a faith mentor can alter a lesson slightly to help keep his or her student engaged for longer periods of time. The "shifting" of the lesson at these moments appears to lead to a better understanding, as evidenced by both the mentee's overall understanding and his or her responses to what is being taught. In most instances, the students with autism are able to communicate the essence of a lesson to me and to their own parents in a clear and astute way.

Ironically, when neurotypical teenagers first begin working with teens or children with autism, they do not seem to have preconceived notions about how they are supposed to respond to their mentees or how to teach/play/interact with them. As a result, teen mentors often react in a more typical fashion to their partners, which seems to have led to a high degree of educational and social learning on the part of the students with autism in my program.

Of course, the pairing of an older student with a younger student in a school setting can present a difficult scheduling problem. Sometimes, using the mentor for a specific class or nonstructured events, such as lunchtime or recess, might be a way to start. With this type of help from a near-aged peer, the overall self-esteem of the child with autism seems to become enhanced. The typical teen, too, seems to grow or mature as a result of having been given the genuine responsibility of caring for another person in a very real sense. It seems to me that both the student with autism and the peer mentor are truly what St. Lawrence referred to as the "treasures of the church."

Summary

Teen and similar-aged peer mentors can be valuable tools and resources for students with autism (and especially for their teachers). A mentor's primary responsibility is to help one specific student, not the whole class. Mentors are often so dedicated to helping their students in whatever way they can that they typically learn successfully and rapidly how to communicate with their mentees. Possibly because of the increased responsibility given to them, the mentors will most often overly prepare by reviewing and learning their students' materials. This is of great benefit to the students with autism. Although teen and peer mentors aren't always panaceas for classroom management or educational needs, they can be invaluable resources to students with autism, while at the same time freeing up teachers to focus on the classroom as a whole.

8

Things That I Can Control

If you are a teacher reading this, one of the questions that might arise is, "What can I do to better understand how children with autism learn so that I can adapt and help them to reach their fullest potential?" This question forms the basis of this chapter.

As a teacher, it is important to understand that you have control over the following:

1. How you use language in the classroom
2. How you set up the classroom
3. How the rules you establish will be enforced in the classroom
4. How you deal with sensory issues within the classroom
5. How much and what type of homework you assign
6. How you get to know your students

Here are some simple strategies that teachers can use to increase the control of their classroom.

How You Use Language in the Classroom

Early in my career, I learned that talking with a child with autism has its own rules. Many children with autism understand language in a literal and concrete way.

If I were to say, "It's raining cats and dogs," in the middle of a downpour, a child with autism might run to the window looking for the cats or dogs falling from the sky and then become angry at me for lying to him or her. That is because he/she did not understand that my expression was a metaphor to express that it was raining very hard. In a similar way, telling children with autism to "wait a minute" can be awfully frustrating for them because they will likely watch a clock and count the seconds until a minute has passed, and sometimes "a minute" might mean a little longer.

Children with autism often have such a difficult time making friends that they will typically do or say anything to make a friend, leaving themselves susceptible to a "designing other"—someone who will take advantage of them. Children with autism often understand language in a literal sense and believe everything they hear from authority figures, such as the teacher, or from trusted peers. For better or worse, fellow students are considered trusted "friends" until one of those "friends" does something hurtful to the child. As noted earlier, children with autism are very literal people, and literal interpretations of a word or phrase may make them easy marks for other children to tease or bully them. Sadly, this type of bullying behavior is very common and often difficult to notice before the damage is done. It is critical that as a teacher, you

- try to be as aware as possible of what might be going on between children with autism and neurotypical peers;
- attempt to understand exactly what has happened when an unfortunate event involving children with autism occurs; and
- speak with the child with autism after such events only after the child has settled or calmed down. This way you can more easily investigate what really occurred.

How You Set Up the Classroom

Many children with autism are easily distracted, particularly when a nonpreferred subject is being taught. As a result, keeping the children focused on your lesson is critical. A teacher can do several things to minimize distractions in a classroom, including some of the following.

Visual Distractions. Keep your classroom *organized*, and keep hangings and pictures in your classroom to a minimum. A cluttered classroom makes it difficult for a child with autism to focus on the teacher. For example, look at the picture on the following page. The room pictured has hangings to the left and right of the whiteboard, and even banners hanging from the ceiling. The room is too cluttered for any child to ever maintain his or her attention on the teacher. The teacher's desk is to one side but distracts from the view because of the amount of clutter on it. Also, there is no clear front to the room.

The classroom in the picture below, however, is far more organized. There are fewer distractions, which makes it much easier for a child with autism to pay close attention to the teacher. Notice that the teacher in this classroom has placed a small bookcase to the side of the only window, minimizing any visual distractions coming from the outside. Notice, as well, that the focus is toward the center of the room. A child with autism can be seated directly in front of the teacher, again minimizing distractions. Finally, the aisle in the center of the room is wide enough to accommodate the teacher's movements and children who need to get up and move around or who will benefit from alternate seating options.

Noise. Noise can be another factor that causes distraction in the classroom. Although carpeting in classrooms can help to minimize noise, sometimes something as simple as using old tennis balls on the bottoms of chair legs can keep unwanted sounds at bay when a room is not carpeted.

Noise and visual distractions are difficult to avoid, and it is imperative that a student with autism have the opportunity to take an exam with as little distraction as possible. Noise-canceling headphones, individual partitions, or study carrels can be very valuable.

How Rules You Establish Will Be Enforced in the Classroom

As noted in chapter 3, children with autism thrive when rules are concrete, clear, and reinforced. If a teacher announces on the first day of class that a student may or may not do some type of activity, then that rule must be enforced going forward. If not, the student with autism could very well have a tantrum or a meltdown. Any change to a rule must be explained fully before enacting any new routine.

One year, when I was assisting Susie before the start of first grade, I had her and her family visit the classroom before the semester began. Susie and her mother were able to meet her teacher as well as her principal. Susie's teacher showed Susie her desk and went over the schedule for a typical day. She also gave her a copy of the school schedule, beautifully decorated with bright colors and images. Susie left her first school visit very happy. When school began, much to her mother's surprise, Susie did well. Although the noise and the number of children, which still caused some confusion, did initially bother her, Susie knew what to expect each day, and the school year began much better than expected.

Susie's story demonstrates that it is critical, especially at the start of a school year, to *create a routine* for students with autism. When possible, this routine should be made into a calendar—a picture calendar, if possible—so that every child understands what is going to happen on a particular day or week. In this way, even for a child who may not be able to tell time, the use of such visual representations of the day's sequence will indicate when something is to end and when a new activity is to begin.

For children with autism, as for many of us, *rules are rules*, and they must be followed. Children with autism may not like a rule, but rules provide the order and structure they need. Many children with autism are not able to plan or organize their day on their own, so they rely on caregivers, especially their teachers, to provide a schedule and an order to the events of their day. Thus, when schedules and routines change, especially at the last minute, meltdowns and temper tantrums are likely to follow. These outbursts are not the children's fault. Many of the changes in a daily routine can be anticipated. Therefore, they need to be explained as soon as possible, both by explaining the change to the class *and* by updating a visual schedule on the white board at the front of the classroom to minimize the disruption for the child with autism.

Inevitably, last-minute changes to routines are sometimes necessary. If the children with autism know that a teacher consistently informs students of surprises and changes *and* makes the corresponding change to the visual calendar as soon as possible *and* explains the reason for doing so, the children with autism may not be happy, but they will be better equipped to manage unexpected deviations to routines when they occur.

How You Deal with Sensory Issues within the Classroom

Teachers typically do not have a lot of control over lighting, temperature, and sound in their classrooms. It is still important, however, to remain mindful of these conditions to help manage sensory overload when possible.

Sound and Light

Most students are not bothered by the buzzing sound being emitted from fluorescent lights. Yet children with autism can be sensitive to this noise, which can lead them to discomfort or distraction. In a similar sense, noise from a fan, either a free-standing fan, the vents of a heating system, or the subtle cooling fan in a computer can be very distracting to some children with autism. Managing these types of sounds may include use of natural light from windows when possible or using other types of light (from lamps) that do not require fluorescent tube bulbs. Seating a child away from a noisy fan or projector might also be helpful. Also, forewarning children with autism when announcements over the school intercom might take place will help them anticipate those loud sounds. Fire drills are another concern. Practicing what to do in that situation individually with children who have autism is critical. It is

important to inform children with autism when a fire drill is scheduled to occur so that they can prepare for it. Knowing what to do in those situations is essential and can include the use of noise-canceling or quieting headphones.

Movement

Many children moving at once can be both distracting and noisy. Having a clear plan of when it is time to move or assemble within the classroom, as well as reinforcing that schedule over time, can lead to a more organized movement and less overall confusion for children with autism. Having rules for who is first in line or last in line when moving is also vital. Often, children with autism wish to please their teacher and so may wish to be first in line. Having a plan in place in advance for who is first in line may also be a critical part of the class movement plan.

Sometimes children with autism become restless and need to stand up and move around. Many times, those same children with autism do not want to stand out, but they still feel fidgety, which in the end causes stress that can lead to an outburst or a meltdown.

One possible solution for managing restlessness in a child with autism is to give the child a sensory break. A teacher can send him or her to other places in the school to run errands for the teacher. I recommend that the child with autism be asked to take a travel pass or a note to the principal's office, deliver a message to the school nurse, or perform some routine job that allows the child to walk and to change his or her environment for a brief period and with a purpose. Doing this twice in the morning and twice in the afternoon would be ideal. In this way, the child learns simple and benign methods to manage restlessness. With older students who are often reluctant to stand out and don't want to be asked to leave, I work with the teacher to have these students hold up coupons or a card (a form of a Travel Pass), signaling to the teacher that the students need a walking break and, without question (depending upon the teachers discretion based on the classroom circumstance), a student can get up and go to a predefined place for a short, finite period of time. I often recommend that older (secondary) students use three of these breaks a day. Once the teacher and student agree on such breaks, it's important for the student to use them each day and to *learn* when it is best to use them (to prioritize times or situations when the travel pass is best used to manage their restlessness or stress or boredom). Some students believe they can manage without breaks—that is, until they can't—so it is important for them to learn their limits and be reassured that it is okay to take a break when they need it.

Sometimes children with autism seem to be restless all the time and just can't sit or keep their hands still. Often, *squirmy cushions* on desk chairs can work well as they do not typically make noise and yet allow students to move back and forth without leaving their desk. Another idea that can often be helpful is attaching the hook portion of hook-and-loop patches under the bottoms of students' desks. The children can then run their fingers over the rough surface, which can do a lot to help ease the need to shift or make broad movements. It can also be helpful for students to use a rosary or a set of worry beads when feeling anxious or fitful. Neither makes much noise, which helps the child's movements to remain anonymous or less noticeable.

The Amount and Type of Homework You Assign

Ashley came home from school Wednesday afternoon singing her favorite song. All signs indicated that she was in a good mood. As it was a couple of hours before dinner, Ashley's mother asked if the two of them could begin working on Ashley's science homework. Her mother knew that Ashley was struggling in science that year. Well, that simple question changed the dynamics in the home for the rest of the evening. Ashley's difficulties with her science homework lead to tantrums, screaming, and screeching that lasted for hours. At nine thirty in the evening, the assignment was abandoned. A tearful Ashley went to bed, and her mother completed the assignment for her.

In routine evaluations, homework is often one of the biggest problems, especially with younger students. When approaching homework that involves new information, a child with autism can struggle for hours to try to complete a task, even with a parent's help. One of the difficulties here is the simple fact that the parent wasn't present when material was discussed and taught. Since children with autism favor routine, there is no way a mom or dad can replicate the material *exactly* as a teacher did earlier in the day. And since children with autism struggle with generalizing concepts, they have great difficulty or are unable to extend their understanding to new information, even if it is based on the same principle.

I feel that children need to do at least some homework each day after returning home; however, this homework should be a review of *learned* material. Homework on new information or new material ideally should be completed while the child has access to the teacher who taught it or gave the assignment. That way, if there is any misunderstanding of how to do something, the teacher can clarify the assignment and assist with understanding how to complete it. In other words, homework on new information or material should be completed while children are still in school and have access to their teacher, while more routine homework can be sent home to be completed.

Children with autism often learn new information through observation, practice, trial and error, and positive reinforcement. Unfortunately, not being present in the classroom when a new subject is introduced, as was the case with Ashley's mother, results in a lack of understanding of the nuances on how the subject was introduced or explained. Ashley's poor mother could never get it right so that Ashley could understand the material.

Once Ashley has grasped the procedure needed to comprehend the material, homework has a valuable place in Ashley's overall learning, for her parents could then help her to both understand the material and to generalize the understanding to other similar topics and materials.

Another common problem occurs when a student completes his homework, but it somehow never makes it back to the teacher. This is often due to the child's organizational difficulties. Brian, for example, completes every assignment on time. Somehow though, his teacher never gets to see his homework, and Brian's grades are unnecessarily lower because he doesn't

hand in his work. This causes great concern for Brian's mother. She sits with Brian each evening as he works on his daily assignments and watches him put the work in his backpack. After the report from his teacher about her not getting the homework, Brian's mom and his teacher sit with Brian and first begin to clean up/look through his backpack. They soon discover most of the semester's completed homework assignments in his backpack.

They then went to his school locker and found dated school materials there, including a permission slip for a recent field trip that was thought to be lost. Although in hindsight these concerns could have been effectively addressed with a little investigation, the problem was ultimately solved between the teacher and Brian's parents. Brian began using colored folders that were checked each day by both his parents and the teacher. It took an entire semester of grief and misunderstanding before the problem was discovered and addressed. In the end, the problem was not Brian acting lazy, it was an issue of executive function.

It seems that the inability to plan and organize, or to do multiple sequential problem-solving tasks, may be *lifelong problems* for individuals with autism. They often need to learn to manage this type of problem by carrying a pocket notebook or similar type of device where assignments and instructions are written down verbatim. Or another method would be for teachers write out homework assignments for students with autism.

How You Get to Know Your Students

Although it may be a cliché, the better I know the child I am working with, the better treatment I can provide for him or her. In a similar sense, the better that teachers know their students, particularly those with autism, the better they can respond to their needs, especially during times of change. As with all children, children with autism grow when they try, learn, and practice new things, whether new math equations, vocabulary, or even fun activities like dancing. When children with autism try new things, they then need fresh scripts or methods to attend to an unfamiliar situation. When they have tried the new activity and acquired the new scripts, they then need to practice in order to feel more comfortable with the new task at hand.

I have found that I can often tell when a child is becoming upset well before there are physical signs, because I make it a point to get to know students really well. I try to understand who a child is, how he or she thinks, and what is important to him or her. Further, I try to understand what actions, behaviors, and sensory problems may lead to a meltdown and which are present in a particular child. Recognizing how a child with autism learns, and incorporating his or her particular learning style into a lesson, can often help the student better understand new material and reduce the likelihood of a meltdown.

Summary

This chapter was included in part to demonstrate that a teacher has many of the tools in his or her classroom that are necessary to help a child with autism successfully learn. Many of the ideas outlined above are commonsense methods predicated upon a teacher *knowing* his or her students. The better a teacher knows the students, the better he or she can anticipate the students' needs.

Methods for helping a child with autism manage a school day can be very simple. Essentially, be aware, communicate, have a plan, follow a daily routine, and make sure you explain changes to schedules in a clear, compassionate, and transparent way. If something goes wrong, don't panic; take appropriate action, communicate, and realize that today is today, tomorrow is tomorrow, and this, too, shall pass.

9

Autism and Coexisting Conditions: What Teachers Need to Know

It is important for teachers to recognize that their primary role with their students is being their educators. Teachers are not meant to be therapists, though they are meant to be helpful and supportive. Teachers help students learn new material as well as develop their capabilities. However, as I have stressed in this book, it is also important to understand that good teachers know their students and are generally able to notice when there is a problem. In this chapter, case examples of different problematic, as well as positive, situations are offered to help teachers detect when something might be wrong, or when something has the potential for good outcomes with one of their students who has autism. Here are some of those situations.

Bullying

Bullying behavior in this context is defined very broadly. It includes physical and verbal aggressions over a prolonged period of time, taking advantage of a child's innocence or trust, neglect from peers, or other subtle methods of excluding a child in activities or social interaction.

Other forms of bullying behavior that children with autism are exposed to may be somewhat more subtle, but the results are often severe. Such was the case with Jimmy. Jimmy is hypersensitive to noise, especially repetitive noises that he cannot control. His sensitivity is such a problem that he wears headphones when he is in the cafeteria or in the auditorium. In one instance of this type of bullying behavior, a classmate named George, who sat directly behind Jimmy, wasn't prepared for the surprise quiz that the teacher was about to distribute to the class. Knowing that Jimmy had problems with noise, George began to softly tap the back of Jimmy's chair with his pencil, knowing that Jimmy would become upset by it. George did this in such a way that the teacher could not see or hear him doing it. The result was predictable. Jimmy soon "exploded" into a meltdown and the teacher was forced to take him to the office for help. By the time the teacher returned, she informed the class that there was no longer enough time for the quiz, and it would need to be postponed until the next day. This not only caused problems on many levels for Jimmy, his teacher, and the class, but the events in question reinforced George's behavior with Jimmy: pick on the kid with autism to derail the class when tests are about to happen.

Eventually, Jimmy had trouble becoming settled in certain classes because he did not know when he would be on the receiving end of George's attacks, and he began having more visible symptoms of anxiety and depression. When children with autism encounter repeated instances of bullying, they, like many other children, seem to stay in a state of hyperalertness, ready for the next problem or assault to occur.

There are many problems that a child with autism can have or may develop over the course of his elementary and secondary education that a teacher who really knows his or her students might be able to recognize. As noted above, the job of a teacher is focused on educating children, not treating them. Identifying changes in mood or behavior or other problems and informing a child's parents before the problems become learning impediments will help the child with autism, the other students, and the teacher as well.

In some instances, a teacher may find that by the time a student gets into secondary education, he or she may have exceptional abilities in certain areas, savant-like or gifted skills in one or more subjects. These need to be supported and reinforced (for these are often the foundation stones for lifelong vocations). However, when the child or teen with autism has become so guarded for fear of being set up to be teased or bullied by his or her classmates or peers, he or she may be too afraid to show or display any of these gifts and talents for fear of being hurt in some fashion by another student.

Depression

The Centers for Disease Control and Prevention (CDC) estimates that more than one out of twenty American children twelve years of age and older experience depression in some form or another. Children and teens with disabilities have an even higher rate of depression. Depression can interfere with the child's ability to do or manage daily activities, such as sleeping, eating, or schoolwork.

Common signs of depression in *typical children* and teens may include visible signs of sadness and empty feelings, hopelessness and feeling as if everything is going wrong, feelings of helplessness or feelings of worthlessness, as well as irritability and isolation. For many children with depression, favorite activities drop away because of a loss of interest or pleasure; sleeping and eating patterns are impaired. They may have trouble sleeping or feel tired all the time; they may have trouble concentrating and have many "pains" in their bodies, especially headaches and stomach problems, and they may have begun to consider suicide as a less painful way or an option for addressing their problems.

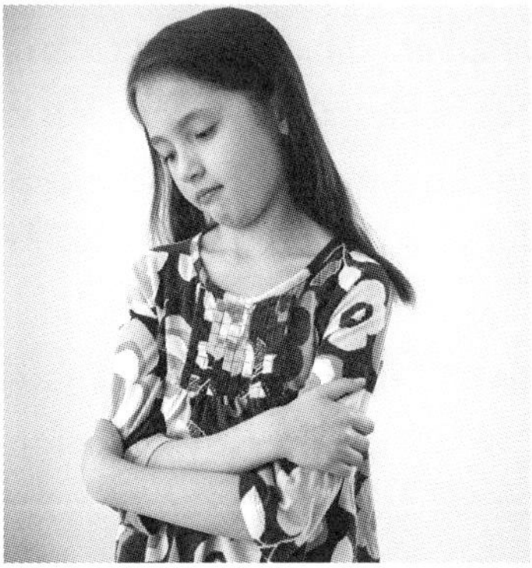

Children and teens with autism may have the same depressive feelings and symptoms that their typical counterparts do, but *they do not show them* by (verbal) complaint, through facial expressions, or through gross visual signs. That is, children and teens with autism who suffer from depression often tend to dress and groom *the same as they typically do.* They do not seek out or ask for help; they do not typically complain about problems with sleep or with having less—or more—appetite. Even when asked directly how they are feeling, *children and teens with autism may not know how to answer,* unless their caregivers (parents or teachers) ask them very specific questions. Fourteen year old Amelia did not acknowledge being more or less hungry than normal over the past 60 days, but she did mention, when asked specifically, that she had dropped twelve pounds in the past 60 days, even though she was not on a diet. This was very important information to notice about the physical effects of her mental state. Other examples might include asking the child how many times he or she may have woken up the night before, or asking about stomach problems they may be experiencing. These are a more effective ways to get to know about the difficulties the child may be experiencing. Children and teens with autism do not often show conventional *vegetative signs of depression* (the symptoms outlined above) until the symptoms are so severe that situations are often life threatening. Knowing the child and asking specific questions relating to depression and suicidal ideation are often necessary (and best) for all children and teens, but especially for those with autism.

Anxiety

Similar to depression, children and teens with autism often suffer from symptoms of anxiety, including feelings of restlessness or "being keyed up." Students with anxiety issues may tire easily, have difficulty concentrating on lessons (even during favorite classes), or experience bouts of irritability and severe worrying. A child often displays anxiety by being easily startled, by nervous hand movements, or by picking behaviors (picking at scabs on their face or arms for example), or by rocking behaviors. These would exceed a child's normal stimming behaviors, if those are normally present. They often worry about things that they have little to no control over. It is important for a teacher to recognize *changes* in a child's behavior and to contact the child's parent or guardian if the changes in behavior continue.

Josh, a boy of thirteen, heard a news report about tornadoes going through the Midwest. He was afraid that the storms might move east and affect him in his home in western Pennsylvania (an area of the country that seldom had tornadoes). Night after night, Josh would watch the evening and late-night news on television for the reports of stormy weather. It became especially bad during hurricane season at the end of the summer, when the weather forecast predicted storms moving northward through the Gulf Coast. Western Pennsylvania would often be the recipient of heavy rain and powerful winds, but rarely hurricane force winds. Still, the threat of hurricanes loomed large for Josh.

Josh's symptoms became so severe at one point that if he was playing outdoors and saw a rain cloud in the sky (a frequent occurrence in areas around Pittsburgh), he'd run into the house and down to the basement for safety. At the time, his parents and I tried to help with alternative methods for him to seek protection. We suggested that Josh check with an authority on the status of the wind and the weather, such as a city parks administrator, or to work with his science teacher in school to learn more about meteorology so that he could "intellectually" understand how tornadoes were formed. However, nothing seemed to help, and Josh inched closer and closer to a full-blown phobia of the wind. Eventually, we sought help from a child psychiatrist who, with prescription medicine and good cognitive behavioral therapy, helped to assuage Josh's fears. The combination of the therapy and medication helped Josh to better manage his anxiety. Although to this day he is clearly anxious when the wind picks up, he no longer has to run into his home to seek shelter in the basement.

Sometimes children and teens display their anxiety through psychomotor movements, such as fidgeting or waving of their hands and fingers. Sometimes they will pick at things, including scabs or sores on their skin or at threads on their clothing, or they may twirl their hair (sometimes to the point of pulling out chunks of it [Trichotillomania]). As mentioned in the section on sensory issues in chapter 8, I often suggest to children with anxiety, their parents, and their teachers that they consider using hook-and-loop patches under their desks for the children to touch or rub or that they hold and touch a rosary or a set of worry beads, which are often a quiet way to do something with one's hands. It is important that as the child's teacher, when you become aware of changes in the child's behavior, you note the changes you've observed and share those observations with the child's parent.

Delayed Development

Because of a delay in overall development, children with autism may be behind in certain areas of growth while other areas are age appropriate. They may appear awkward or clumsy in some physical activities that require gross motor coordination and yet are gifted in other areas. Fine motor delays are possible as well. For example, these students may need ongoing occupational therapy for their handwriting to be legible. Recognizing that these delays might be caused by *developmental delays or problems*, a teacher could make appropriate accommodations or modifications. These might include not requiring the child to perform in ways that their physical limitations prevent and/or making reasonable accommodations that capitalize on areas of potential strengths, such as using a word processor or speech-to-text computer programs to facilitate written and verbal communication.

It is also important to remember that it's often difficult to ascertain what a child with autism knows and doesn't know. Consider Greg. He is a young man now, but when he was starting school at age five, he had a measured intelligence quotient of 64, a score in the mild range of intellectual impairment. Still, Greg was a child who had relatively good expressive language and did not have notable behavioral problems. This allowed him to attend a typical kindergarten program. Yet, though Greg was enrolled in the school, he was pretty much invisible in the classroom. He did not volunteer answers until asked by his teachers, and he socialized little with his fellow students. When Greg turned eighteen years old, he participated in a second cognitive evaluation to see if he met the requirements to receive a form of Social Security Disability. Greg's measured intelligence at that time was 72—both this testing result and the testing conducted when he was five years of age were considered valid to be deemed to have a disability. At age twenty-one years, Greg finished secondary education and was approached by the Office of Vocational Rehabilitation (a federal program available in each state, although some states may identify it by a different name.) Now Greg participated in a third cognitive evaluation and his measured intelligence was 94, a score in the average range of measured intelligence. This test, like the previous two, was also considered valid for judging his eligibility to receive disability benefits.

In Greg's situation, the information processing impairment resulting from his developmental disorder seemed to have lessened as he got older. My personal understanding was that over time, Greg became more efficient in processing problems typically included on tests in general, including typical cognitive tests. To me it meant, in part, that

Greg was always as intelligent as his most recent results showed. It was just that now the instruments seemed better able to measure his actual intelligence and problem solving abilities.

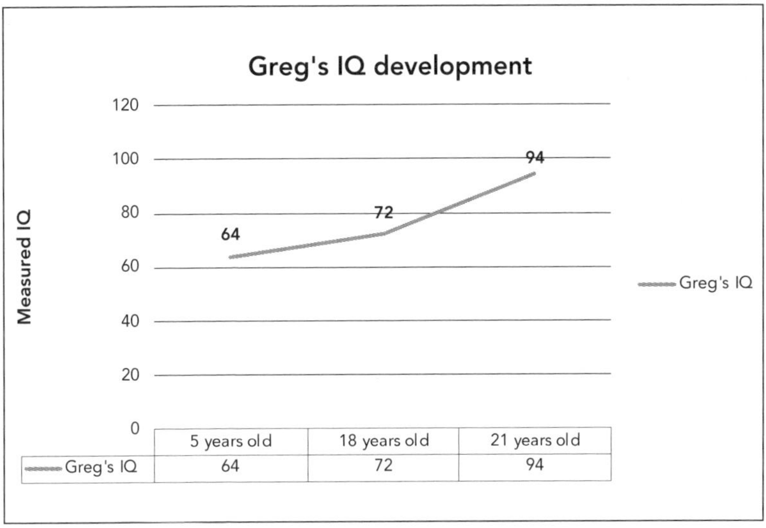

Although this type of change in measured intelligence isn't common, delays seem to sometimes be the result of the *slow processing of information*, which may, in some cases, become less impairing over time with some children and teens who have autism. Teachers of these students need to allow for the possibility of such changes and make routine and regular adjustments in the child's educational plan to reflect changes in the student's abilities.

When educating children with autism, it is important not to make finalized or permanent assumptions about what they can or cannot do or learn, particularly when those assumptions are based on information gathered early in the child's life.

Trauma

Teachers are not psychologists, but it is important to recognize that when seemingly benign events lead a child with autism to angry outbursts, there is almost always a trigger for something deeper. A child may hear, see, or smell something in passing that prompts a recollection of a traumatic event. Although trauma is not a co-occurring disorder for children and teens with autism, traumatic events do seem to occur with some frequency to them. Quick and sometimes dramatic changes in a child's response to a song being played in the classroom, for example, may be related to some other event that had a strong impact on the child. Sometimes changes in mood or behavior may be caused by seemingly unrelated events that occurred near to or in direct contact to children with autism. When this occurs, it is important that those people who spend time with these children pay attention to the children's behavior. When a teacher recognizes this type of response, it is important to be patient and compassionate, to note the action that caused the reaction, and report it to the child's parents.

Giftedness

As discussed earlier, some children and teens with autism have savant-like or highly gifted abilities in one or more areas. Sometimes these gifts are pervasive, and the child may qualify for gifted education. Many more times, however, a child may have enhanced gifts in specific subjects and the skills he or she demonstrates need to be encouraged and supported by their teachers. It is to these children that specialized enrichment is even more important, as specific skills demonstrated as a young child might lead to a vocation as an adult.

Take James, for example. James was seven years old when I evaluated him. He had many behavioral and sensory symptoms of autism, which required direct in-home intervention. James also had an interest in and an apparent gift for art and drawing. I noticed during my evaluation with him that James would doodle. His doodles were impressive for his age. His parents agreed, but they were concerned that he spent too much time doodling instead of doing other activities, including his schoolwork. In class, when James would start his doodles, other students would gather around his desk, and his parents were afraid that encouraging James to draw might be even more disruptive to his classwork. At the time of the evaluation, summer break was approaching, and I asked James's parents if they might consider engaging the school art teacher, who was not working over the summer break, to see if she would be interested in working with their son over the next few months. The thought was to see if the art teacher *could enhance, not change*, the work that James was doing with his drawings. It turned out that they took me up on my suggestion. Eleven years later I attended James's graduation party from high school. In the room where the celebration took place were dozens of James' drawings. They were amazing works of art! Moreover, I learned that James had been accepted to a prestigious art school (he couldn't enroll in a regular college because his performance in other subjects was not as strong as were his gifts in art). His gift in art had flourished into a future as an artist.

The following example happened with a neurotypical teen, but I want to share it because it represents a possibility that would have great results for students with autism. There is no reason a student with autism who is gifted in math or another subject could not benefit from this sort of intervention. Furthermore, the private Catholic school setting might be an ideal place to execute this kind of plan. Andrew is an example of a child who excelled in everything related to mathematics. Unlike James, Andrew was good in all his subjects in school, but he especially loved math. As he grew, the principal of his small Catholic school recognized his interest and gifts with numbers. The principal asked one of the teachers who, herself had been considered gifted in math when she was in school, to organize a special math group. She more than obliged. Andrew was one of four students chosen for the group. That year, the school entered the State of Pennsylvania Algebra tournament—and won, despite competing with other Catholic schools, private prep schools, and other highly specialized public-school academies. Andrew, as it turned out, had the highest score in the state. Andrew later attended university and graduated with a degree in statistics. Today he is working successfully in a competitive finance area, thanks in large part to an insightful Catholic school principal and a caring algebra teacher.

Recognizing and honoring the special gifts of any children, but especially children with autism, can sometimes lead those individuals to an enhanced quality of life and to employment in a vocation that they truly love.

Adolescence

Is adolescence a condition that requires an intervention? Though it might feel like it sometimes—with hormonal changes, mood swings, bad attitudes, and sometimes aggressive behavior—adolescence is not a disorder; but it is a time when it seems all the rules in life are changing. This, of course, can make it an even more difficult time for those with autism. Almost overnight, a child's body starts to change and do odd things. Peers begin acting differently. High emotions are labile for young adolescents both with and without autism, and no one acts the way they did before. Children with autism, who depend on uniformity and are bothered by change, often feel lost during adolescence. Further, they are often not able to communicate to someone else what would help make things better for them.

In a similar sense, teens who have autism aren't typically able to anticipate change. They often lack insight and don't generalize learned things to new situations when something similar occurs. It is important that teachers make sure that their students with autism really understand changes in routine and when possible provide context or reasons for why change is occurring.

Take Daniel for example. Daniel did not have a lot of friends, but several of his peers had been close to him since he was a toddler. Daniel came home from school one day and asked his mother why Mary, a girl who was a real friend to Daniel, and had known him since they were very young, didn't like him anymore. He went on to say that she started hitting him in the shoulder at lunch in the school cafeteria, and when he told her to stop, she kept doing it. To make matters worse, she giggled while she was hitting him. Daniel asked his mother, "Why does Mary hate me?" having concluded that she must hate him because she was hitting him. Daniel did not recognize that the change in Mary's behavior was the result of changes that can occur during adolescence. In this case, Mary might have been displaying a type of "precourtship" behavior when she was striking him and may have been trying to convey that she liked him in a romantic way. But Daniel understood it differently and thought she was angry with him. Now, it isn't the job of a teacher to be a matchmaker for his or her students; however, when such a scene is recognized for what it is, and one of the parties—in this case, Daniel—isn't understanding what is really going on, then explaining what might really be the case could help to ease hurt feelings.

It is particularly important that during adolescence, when human sexuality issues start to surface, adults take time to help teens with autism navigate the emotional ups and downs that are part of growing up. Teens with autism have interest in human sexuality similar to their peers, but they most often don't understand either what the interest means or how to express it. They don't know how to ask questions and are afraid of some of their bodily changes. Before adolescence, they may have looked to their peers to find out how to act or what to do in various school situations. But precourtship and courtship types of rituals are particularly difficult for teens who still struggle with knowing how to make friends or even how to carry on basic social conversations.

Teachers can assist with some of the adolescent questions by anticipating and modeling how to ask them or how to respond. For example, Daniel's teacher might suggest that he ask Mary, "Why are you hitting me on my shoulder? Are you mad at me?" Or, "When you hit me on the shoulder, are you upset with me, or does it mean something else?" Knowing something is different and knowing how to figure out the change can be a daunting task for someone with autism. A little help can be very beneficial.

Summary

Children and teens with autism aren't immune to problems each of us face every day, including feelings of uncertainty, low self-esteem, anxiety, and even depression.

Although Catholic school teachers are not psychologists or behavioral clinicians, they are a compassionate Christian people who care for their students. Teachers pray with their students and know them as individuals. Teachers are often the first to recognize when something is different with their students. And although they may not always know what to do at the time to help their students in need, most teachers strive to learn more so they can help and support them as their needs arise.

Children and teens with autism are in so many ways the same as other Catholic school students. They need teachers who proactively work with them to bring out their God-given gifts so that, in the bigger picture, they will end up as happy, productive adults.

Words of Encouragement

Catholic schools are built to serve all God's children. Their mission and very structure call teachers and staff to assist and be there for all. Children with disabling conditions like autism need help to reach their cognitive, physical, and spiritual potentials. They need good teachers to help them thrive!

As I sit here writing this note, I can't help but think about those children I met as young toddlers and continue to interact with as adults. I could never have imagined when they were young how much they would grow and develop over the years. Some of these individuals were educated in public schools and some in Catholic schools. Many of those who succeeded as young adults grew up in environments where their personal, God-given gifts were allowed to blossom and develop. As autism is a lifelong developmental disorder, even the most successful of those I've worked with in the past still need help and direction when faced with new situations and challenges in their jobs and personal relationships, including marriage and parenthood. Though everyone is different in terms of cognitive faculties, those who were fortunate enough to have astute and caring teachers in their lives almost always excelled in some way.

Teaching a child who has autism, or any child with a disabling condition, in a Catholic school provides a unique opportunity, not only for the child with the disabling condition but also for each of his or her classmates. For by allowing a safe and supportive environment for children with autism to grow, these children's personal gifts end up enriching everyone around them. As we are called to reach out and help those in need and those who can't do what others can, we must act with intention. As noted earlier, children and teens with autism often require a slightly different approach to learning. Some need to visualize things in order to understand and move forward, while others may need to methodically move forward in incremental steps. Many of the Catholic school teachers I have met and worked with seem to understand and are more than willing to present material in a slightly different way to help a child comprehend a given topic more fully.

I hope this book has provided you with ideas and context to consider when working with, interacting with, and teaching children and teens with autism. There are a lot of children like Mark (described in chapter 1), who are entering our Catholic schools. They are looking for clear and structured environments in which to learn and where they can feel cared for while exploring the ultimately beautiful world around them. Catholic schools really help children to enrich the gifts that God has given each of them, thus allowing them to share these gifts with the world. One of my challenges in preparing this book was to remember that as a clinician, I was writing to teachers about teaching. It is my hope that as a teacher you will take away the following points:

1. Autism spectrum disorders are complex and varied. Knowing the name of the disorder doesn't necessarily tell you much, or at least not enough about the specific student, if you're going to be an effective teacher for that student.
2. The better you know a child and understand how he or she communicates and solves problems, the better he or she will learn in your classroom.
3. Students with autism vary greatly. Some are distracted by noise or by movement, and some have to have material presented in a specific way. They are often very different from one another,

and as a result, you may not be able to generalize your teaching strategy to all. Instead, you may need to create an individual approach or style for each of your students who have autism.

4. There are often simple behavioral methods to help identify when a child with autism might have a meltdown or a behavioral problem. There are methods for understanding what that child might be trying to say by displaying a behavior. Always remember: children with autism often communicate through their behavior.
5. Students with autism aren't immune to having other disorders, and as they move through school, you may have concerns that the student could develop problems with anxiety and/or depression (which often aren't easily recognized in their initial stages). These children may need help with these problems as well.
6. It is important to be alert for how your student with autism relates to and interacts with other students. Students with autism don't always understand how to make or keep friends. They also don't immediately pick up on changes in relationships, so they need help to see what might be obvious to others, such as when they are being teased by someone they thought was a friend or when they are being taken advantage of by a classmate. Further, due in part to sensory problems or rigid rituals, many students with autism are easy marks for being bullied. Students with autism are vulnerable to subtle forms of bullying behaviors from other students, and as a teacher, it is important that you be alert for such behaviors in your classroom.
7. When possible, include a student and his or her preferred interests in your lessons. If a child with autism is an "expert" on an aspect of one of your lessons, intentionally allow him or her

to share this knowledge with your class. This typically leads to heightened self-esteem and self-confidence for the child.

8. Although it may not be something you are accustomed to, using teen mentors with students who have autism can lead to myriad beneficial results for both the student with autism and the mentor. Often when a child with autism has an older student as a mentor, concerns about peer bullying behaviors seem to decrease.
9. Finally, take advantage of available resources from other teachers, the child's parents, and local providers who are willing to offer their services at little or no cost. The education program for students with autism I developed was greatly enhanced when another psychologist, three retired teachers, and a language pathologist became part of the program because they felt a calling to help those in need as *volunteers*.

Having a student with autism in your class is an opportunity for your class to better understand children who have disabling conditions. While I've mentioned this many times, it is important to remember that the child with autism enriches your classroom through his or her personal gifts, and this gives other students the chance to share their gifts as well. Although having a child with autism in your classroom may require you to alter your lesson plans, the modifications are often simple and needn't be complicated.

Thank you, and God bless you for taking the time to learn more about how to educate a child with autism in your classroom. I wish you the very best success!

Deacon Lawrence R. Sutton, Ph.D.

Appendix

Promising Practices in Catholic Schools

Over the past five years, I've had the opportunity to visit many Catholic dioceses in the United States, Canada, the Philippines and in West Africa and to examine a number of promising school programs to address the needs of students with disabilities. Among other things, when I have entered a diocese, I have asked to meet with school personnel—both in elementary and secondary schools. In these meetings I have asked about how children and adolescents with disabling conditions are educated. I have learned that there are some amazing schools with extraordinary programs. Each of these schools has embodied some of the most promising principles and programs that other Catholic schools might consider emulating.

Schools

The following schools are a small sampling of Catholic schools in the United States that strive to use/develop and implement best-practice methods to help the students with autism (and those with other disabling conditions) to succeed.

St. Madeleine Sophie Catholic School, Bellevue, Washington: This school focuses on including students with developmental disabilities from kindergarten through grade eight. At St. Madeleine Sophie, students with autism and/or other developmental disabilities participate in the general education curriculum with "additional curriculums and ancillary materials," which are created by a formal inclusion teacher. Each student in the school has an individual behavior plan. Behavioral issues, including stimming and meltdowns, are handled on an individual basis, regardless of diagnosis. When a student becomes "stuck" on a preferred topic of interest, they are helped by being given specific times each school day to use and express their preferred topic.

At St. Madeleine Sophie, best-practice teaching means a "regular classroom," which is in a fully inclusive environment of all students. "Students are not labeled, their abilities and diagnosis do not define who they are as learners, but rather informs how we teach to best meet their needs. Anything that a teacher does for one student with or without autism is going to benefit all students. Students learn best from each other when they experience their similarities and differences together in one classroom. Teachers create a safe, nurturing environment where each child can learn and grow to know that they are made in the image and likeness of God."

The School at McGuire Memorial, New Brighton, Pennsylvania: This school is part of the ministry of the Felician Sisters of North America. McGuire Memorial is a not-for-profit, nondenominational facility that has, since 1963, served those who are physically and developmentally challenged.

The School at McGuire Memorial is an approved private school for children ages three through twenty-one with disabilities. All students at McGuire have a developmental disability, and the school specializes in teaching children with autism. At McGuire, students are referred and placed by their public school district. When a child is enrolled, additional assessments occur at McGuire. In addition to the classroom teacher's curriculum-based assessments, students may also be assessed by an occupational therapist, physical therapist, speech therapist, and school nurse or behavior analyst. The information gathered from these formal and informal assessments is used to develop an IEP, or Individualized Education Plan.

McGuire's secondary education program, is called the LIFE Academy. LIFE is an acronym for Learning in Functional Environments. LIFE Academy consists of seven functional areas: a fully equipped kitchen, a laundry room, a bedroom, a living room/lounge, a vocational training room, a functional academic room, and a daily living/social skills room. To build in flexibility, the students also change classes. Each student is assigned a homeroom teacher that teaches either daily living skills, vocational training, or functional academics. Following their schedule, the students then rotate to the other teachers throughout the day. Transition activities play a big role in the education of students who are fourteen years and older. They participate in job-training activities in the school, on the campus, and in the community. Using school vans, each classroom participates in community-based instruction at least once a week. The program also uses a unique video-modeling program with iPads to minimize dependency on cues for task completion and maximize independence.

At McGuire Memorial, a child's behavior, whether anger, excitement, or getting "stuck" on a preferred interest is addressed in a Positive Support Plan. Challenging behaviors are identified as those that impede the learning of the child or other students. The goal of the Positive Behavior Support Program is to address behaviors that are *socially significant*. The School uses the function of the challenging behavior to develop goals, replacement behaviors, reinforcement schedules, etc. The school employs *behavior analysts and behavior technicians* who work together to assess challenging behaviors through a Functional Behavior Assessment or Functional Analysis; the function of the behavior drives the treatment. All staff are trained before implementation, and data drives decision making. At McGuire, all education must be individualized, based on state standards, and adapted to the strengths and needs of the learner and must utilize strategies that are evidence-based (i.e., have a strong history of objective evidence in the literature of positive outcomes for the learner), such as those found in the *National Standards Report*, a document published by The National Autism Center, whose goal is to identify evidence-based practices for children with an autism spectrum disorder. This document is divided into sections that identify established treatments, any emerging treatments, and unestablished treatments.

St. Nicholas of Tolentine School, Chicago, Illinois: This elementary school includes children with autism and other developmental disorders from prekindergarten through eighth grade. Students who have an Autism Diagnosis receive ABA Therapy throughout the day. The number of minutes is assigned according to each student's Individualized Educational Plan (IEP). Identified students participate in Title 1 classes, Learning Resource classes that support classroom instruction. At St. Nicholas of Tolentine, the focus is on Inclusion for all with a strong MTSS team that supports the classroom teacher, and outside resources through partnership with Loyola University Chicago. St. Nicholas of Tolentine also uses an inclusion committee that consists of teachers, students, and parents. There is a sensory room for the students and an inclusion director to assist families in understanding their child's needs.

Students at St. Nicholas are full members of the school community, participating in school clubs, sports teams, and music groups. Behavioral issues such as stimming are addressed by the classroom teacher educating, or explaining to, the other students in the classroom what is happening. Often, a student's stimming behavior is eventually accepted by the other students. The teachers also develop and include areas of preferred interest in lessons for the whole class. They use the student's strengths to help the other children in class to achieve success.

Best practices at St. Nicholas of Tolentine School are defined as, "Meet the needs of ALL students through differentiation of instructional practice (whole group, small group, individualized), knowledge of student's learning styles—paired, team and individualized activities with selection of appropriate grade level standards aligned with curricular resources for effective lessons); students are given voice and choice in lessons."

Our Lady of Grace and St. Thomas More Catholic Schools in the Diocese of Pittsburgh, Pennsylvania: Our Lady of Grace Catholic Elementary School gradually included children with autism in each grade over the first 14 years of the autism religious education ministry, which I initiated within that parish. In October 2018, the Diocese of Pittsburgh went into a major parish consolidation, merging some 250 parishes into approximately 50. With good fortune, the autism religious education program at Our Lady of Grace was able to, by my request, join a neighboring parish, St. Thomas More, whose school has a formalized and integrated autism program within it. The autism program now housed at the St. Thomas More Parish, continues to include children and teens with autism spectrum disorders, as well as those with other developmental disorders. The program serves over 20 children per week with over 20 teen mentors. It will soon begin offering services to adults with autism spectrum disorders as well as adults with other developmental disorders, who were once thought to be "too special" to need religious education. This will happen under the new umbrella ministry of the **St. Lawrence Ministry**, recognizing the gifts that all have to offer the Church. If you would like additional information about this program, I can be reached at St. Thomas More Parish at https://www.stmpgh.org or lsutton@diopitt.org

Patrick Speech and Languages Centre, Lagos, Nigeria: This center was created to assist children with autism spectrum Disorders, Asperger's Syndrome (High Functioning forms of Autism), Speech and Language problems, and other developmental learning disabilities. The Centre works with 40 pupils ranging in age from 3 to 40 provides services such as Behavior, Occupational and Speech, Music as well as vocational therapies.

The Treasure Center, Bamenda, Cameroon: The Treasure Center is operated in part by the Holy Rosary Sisters, which provides a safe, happy, and healthy environment where children and young adults with developmental disabilities, including autism and intellectual disabilities, can learn and develop socially, emotionally, and spiritually, while acquiring the skills to function to the best of their abilities in society. The Center works with 152 individuals in need.

Other Resources

The FIRE Foundation, Kansas City, Missouri: The FIRE Foundation is an independent organization that promotes inclusive Catholic education in Catholic schools. Through its grants, the foundation helps Catholic schools hire special educators and paraprofessionals, acquire materials and technology, and promote and create successful learning experiences for all children, especially children on the autism spectrum.

The FIRE Foundation's mission is to "provide children with special needs the opportunity for an inclusive Catholic education in their home parish schools." The Foundation promotes best practices for teaching and supporting students with special needs. It has identified "essential best practices" to include the following:*

- The inherent value, dignity, and competence of students should always be respected.
- Students are welcomed members of their school, with "access to the full range of learning experiences and environments" as anyone else.
- Curriculum and related supports are designed to enable students to participate fully and make progress within the general education classroom, learning within typical routines of the school.
- Necessary supports enhance both academic and social participation.

- Student testing and assessment are performed in their natural context and setting, with the focus on the student's personal best, their strengths, and progress.
- Families and schools form an equitable partnership to create a quality inclusive educational experience.
- General and special-education teachers, as well as paraprofessionals and other support staff, demonstrate shared responsibility for the student's education.
- Friendships and social relationships are parallel goals of inclusive education.
- As appropriate, students are provided with opportunities and the related supports to develop skills such as decision making, problem solving, decision making, and self-advocacy.

Additional Key Indicators*

- Curriculum is presented in a variety of formats (video, pictures, actual objects, demonstrations, electronically, small groups, at the board, etc.)
- Peer supports should be reciprocal: students should have the opportunity to provide support to others as well as receive it.
- Inclusive education thrives within a "schoolwide positive behavior philosophy" rather than a punitive one.
- Family priorities are considered in annual goals.
- School personnel are invested in the connection between social relationships and student learning and use intentional strategies to promote friendships.

* Content is adapted from FIRE Foundation resources and from Cheryl M. Jorgensen, Michael McSheehan, Mary Schuh, and Rae M. Sonnenmeier, *Essential Best Practices in Inclusive Schools* (Durham, N.H.: Institute on Disability, University of New Hampshire, July 2012). Used by permission.

- Opportunities for making authentic and real choices are infused throughout a student's day.
- Predictions that students will "never" acquire certain knowledge or skills are simply not allowed.
- Students' names are on all class lists, group lists, and job lists.

Works Cited

Centers for Disease Control and Prevention. "Children's Mental Health." Children's Mental Health. September 5, 2019. https://www.cdc.gov/childrensmentalhealth/depression.html.

Centers for Disease Control and Prevention. "Data & Statistics on Autism Spectrum Disorder." Autism Spectrum Disorder (ASD). September 3, 2019. https://www.cdc.gov/ncbddd/autism/data.html.

Diagnostic and Statistical Manual of Mental Disorders: Diagnostic and Statistical Manual of Mental Disorders, Fifth Edition. Arlington, VA: American Psychiatric Association, 2013.

Guidelines for the Celebration of the Sacraments with Persons with Disabilities, Revised Edition. Washington, D.C.: United States Conference of Catholic Bishops, 2017.

The Holy Bible, New International Version. Grand Rapids, MI: Zondervan House, 1984.

Jorgensen, Cheryl M., McSheehan, Michael, Schuh, Mary, and Sonnenmeier, Rae M. *Essential Best Practices in Inclusive Schools*. Durham, NH: Institute on Disability, University of New Hampshire, July 2012.

Lori J Marra, MA, CCC-SLP, e-mail message to author, September 18, 2019.

National Directory for Catechesis. Washington, D.C: United States Conference of Catholic Bishops, 2005.

New American Bible, Revised Edition. Charlotte, NC.: Saint Benedict Press, LLC, 2011.

Pope Francis, "Address of his Holiness Pope Francis to participants in the XXIX International Conference sponsored by the Pontifical Council for Health Care Workers on the theme 'The Person with Autism Spectrum Disorders: Animating Hope.'" Address presented at Paul VI Audience Hall, Vatican City, November 22, 2014.

Sutton, Lawrence, *How to Welcome, Include, and Catechize Children with Autism and Other Special Needs: A Parish-Based Approach*. Chicago: Loyola Press, 2013.

Turkson, Cardinal Peter, "World Autism Awareness Day Message." Message Released by the Holy See Press Office, Vatican City, April 2, 2018.

U.S. Department of Health and Human Services. "Bullying and Youth with Disabilities and Special Health Needs." Stopbullying.gov. July 23, 2018. https://www.stopbullying.gov/at-risk/groups/special-needs/index.html

Acknowledgments

In preparing this book, I received a great deal of assistance, inspiration, and support from many sources.

I am grateful to Dan Sherman, Sandy Barton Smith, Erica Cohen Moore, and the teachers at the Madeline Sophie School in Bellevue Washington for their support and inspiration. They challenged me to constantly "push the bar," to believe that nothing is impossible when you have a dedicated and coordinated team. In a similar way, I am so grateful to pastor Richard Infante, and principals Lindsay Pfister and Sharon Brown of Our Lady of Grace, a parish that will never be forgotten, for allowing me to not only think outside the box in the parish school, but also helping me to do it, and joining me in our successes. And a special thanks to Peg Kolm, Mary O'Meara, Peter Ductram, Barbara McAtee and Dennis Johnston.

I am grateful to Mike Boyle for his patient guidance and strict adherence to my style in writing. And, I am very thankful to the team of editors at Loyola Press who help this process to become tangible on paper.

In a fundamental way, I am thankful and grateful to my wife, Nancy, and our children Dan, Brian, Mark, Elizabeth, and Ashley, and to the mentors and students over these many years, each of whom I have referenced here in one way or another in my stories and examples. You are what makes life so very meaningful and worthwhile.

About the Author

Lawrence R. Sutton, Ph.D. is an ordained deacon and a psychologist specializing in developmental disabilities, especially autism spectrum disorders. He is the former Manager of the Western Region Office of the Pennsylvania Bureau of Autism Services and is currently the director of the Pre-Theologian Formation program and teacher at St. Vincent Seminary. He is nationally recognized for developing his own methodology for providing religious education to children with special needs.

Art/Photo Credits

When there is more than one picture on a page, positions are abbreviated as follows: (t) top, (c) center, (b) bottom, (l) left, (r) right, (bg) background, (bd) border.

Chapter 1
8 (br) Dorling Kindersley/Getty Images. **8 (bc)** Weekend Images Inc./E+/Getty Images. **8 (bl)** Iurii Kachkovskyi/Shutterstock.com **7 (br)** arekmalang/iStock/Getty Images. **10** stefanolunardi/Shutterstock.com.

Chapter 2
13 Klaus Vedfelt/DigitalVision/Getty Images. **14 (tl)** AGL_Photography/iStock/Getty Images. **14 (tr)** imagenavi/Getty Images.

Chapter 3
32 sirikorn thamniyom/Shutterstock.com. **33 (a)** ferrantraite/iStock/Getty Images. **33** PhotoAlto/Anne-Sophie Bost/PhotoAlto Agency RF Collections/Getty Images. **35** Caiaimage/Paul Bradbury/Caiaimage/Getty Images.

Chapter 4
38 Warling Studios. **39 (tl)** Loyola Press **39 (tr)** Phil Martin Photography. **41** Creativa Images/Shutterstock.com **43** Maskot/Maskot/Getty Images.

Chapter 5
49 Hero Images/Getty Images. **53** progressman/Shutterstock.com. **53** stocksnapper/iStock/Getty Images.

Chapter 6
58 AMORNTEP/Shutterstock.com. **60 (t)** Parilov/Shutterstock.com. **60 (b)** Bohbeh/Shutterstock.com. **61** Loyola Press. **62** Loyola Press. **65** Loyola Press. **66** Loyola Press. **67** Avaniks/Shutterstock.com.

Chapter 7
69 Image Source Photography/Veer. **71 (a)** Hero Images/Hero Images/Getty Images. **71 (b)** Phil Martin Photography. **72** Pavel L Photo and Video/Shutterstock.com. **73 (t)** paulaphoto/Shutterstock.com. **73 (b)** MilaLiu/Shutterstock.com. **75** FatCamera/E+/Getty Images.

Chapter 8
78 gpointstudio/iStock/Getty Images. **80 (t)** JohnnyGreig/E+/Getty Images. **80 (b)** Serhii Fedoruk/Shutterstock.com. **82 (tl)** Steve Debenport/E+/Getty Images. **82 (tr)** Jose Luis Pelaez Inc/Digital Vision/Getty Images. **82 (cl)** KidStock/Blend Images/Veer. **82 (cr)** Highwaystarz-Photography/iStock/Getty Images. **82 (b)** Lynn Koenig/Moment/Getty Images. **83** Matthias Tunger/DigitalVision/Getty Images. **84** Warling Studios. **86** New Africa/Shutterstock.com. **87** Greg Kuepfer.

Chapter 9
92 (tl) Phil Martin Photography. **92 (tr)** Phil Martin Photography. **94 (tl)** cultura Photography/Veer. **94 (tr)** JGI/Jamie Grill/Veer. **95** vchal/Shutterstock.com. **96 (tl)** urbans/Shutterstock.com. **96 (tr)** Jack Hollingsworth/Photodisc/Getty Images. **99** Loyola Press. **101** JINI SNAP/Shutterstock.com. **104** Sarah Casillas/DigitalVision/Getty Images.